Overcoming Sex Add

C000157097

Overcoming Sex Addiction is an accessible self-help guide which uses the principles of cognitive behaviour therapy to help those with problematic or unwanted patterns of sexual behaviour. It is designed for those who are not yet ready to seek professional help or who live in a place where little help is available and can be used in conjunction with general psychotherapy. Written by a leading expert in the field, the book offers an insight into the origins of sex addiction, before going on to explain the cycle of addiction and how to break it.

The book has a do-it-yourself week-by-week programme of action to tackle compulsive sexual behaviour, and provides extensive advice on relapse prevention to help the reader move forward in recovery.

Overcoming Sex Addiction will provide clear, informed guidance for sex addicts and those professionals working with them.

Thaddeus Birchard is the founder of the Marylebone Centre. He has an MSc in psychosexual therapy and a doctorate in the treatment of hyper-sexual disorders. He is accredited by the British Association for Behavioural and Cognitive Psychotherapies and is the founder of the Association for the Treatment of Sexual Addiction and Compulsivity.

This book has it all for someone struggling with problematic sexual behaviours. It has a thorough but readable background on key points surrounding problematic sexual behaviours. It then has highly effective exercises and plans, with clear examples and explanations. This guide-book is aimed at helping anyone enduring the effects of problematic sexual behaviours to begin and maintain a road of health and wellbeing. Anyone who is living with the trauma of their sexual behaviours will find this book immensely helpful and hopeful.

Dr Mary Deitch, *President of the Society for the Advancement of Sexual Health and owner of Deitch Therapy and Consulting, LLC in Pennsylvania, USA*

Leading UK sex addiction expert, Dr Thaddeus Birchard, shares his specialist knowledge, experience and interventions in sex addiction and gives us something special in this gem of a self-help resource book. A highly recommended read, it is an incisive, instructive and enabling resource to transform the patient into self-therapist in the recovery from sex addiction. The book conveys tremendous empathy, skill and deep understanding of the patient perspective. Peppered throughout with case vignettes, exercises and imparted knowledge, this fantastic resource promotes hope and a sense of connection with others in the pursuit of self-understanding. It explains how to get started and make the journey of recovery towards a healthier life.

Lesley Boswell, *Vice Chairperson of the Association for the Treatment of Sex Addiction and Compulsivity, UK (ATSAC)*

This long-awaited sex addiction self-help guide comes from the power-house of the treatment of sexual addiction, the Marylebone Centre for Psychological Therapies. With this publication, the centre's founder, Dr Thaddeus Birchard, generously shares his wisdom and decades of experiences. The text reviews the field of sexual addiction with a focus on practice-relevant knowledge. Furthermore, the book enhances its readers' self-awareness and alternative coping strategies through a series of well-designed practical exercises, many of which have found their way into treatment programmes for sexual addiction offered in the UK and Europe.

Being the first self-help resource for sexual addiction that is solidly grounded in cognitive mechanisms and treatment evaluation, this resource is not only of interest to all people who struggle with out-of-control sexual behaviours, but also for all therapists who support them.

Dr Tom Werner, *Psychiatrist, Medical Trainer and CBT Therapist working as leader of the Community Mental Health Team at the Maudsley NHS Foundation Trust, UK*

Overcoming Sex Addiction

A Self-Help Guide

Thaddeus Birchard

Routledge
Taylor & Francis Group

LONDON AND NEW YORK

First published 2017
by Routledge
2 Park Square, Milton Park, Abingdon, Oxon OX14 4RN

and by Routledge
711 Third Avenue, New York, NY 10017

Routledge is an imprint of the Taylor & Francis Group, an informa business

© 2017 Thaddeus Birchard

British Library Cataloguing in Publication Data
A catalogue record for this book is available from the British Library

Library of Congress Cataloging in Publication Data
A catalog record for this book has been requested

ISBN: 978-1-138-92533-5 (hbk)
ISBN: 978-1-138-92534-2 (pbk)
ISBN: 978-1-315-67822-1 (ebk)

Typeset in Times New Roman
by Wearset Ltd, Boldon, Tyne and Wear

Contents

Illustrations

Figures

Tables

Part I

Preliminary readings

Chapter 1

Introduction

About this book

This book is designed as a 'do-it-yourself' therapy book for anyone wishing to begin the journey of recovery from sexual addiction. After all, any recovery from addictive behaviours cannot be done by anyone else. Even with a team of the best therapists in the world, you are the only person who can change yourself. When I see addicts, I make the point that you have to want recovery and be willing to put in the time, energy and thought that is required to make the change. All that I can do is to provide support, insight and answers to questions; well, maybe a little more, because having someone who is working with you and rooting for you helps to increase motivation. But this book is designed for people who are not able to access recovery-oriented therapy or who simply cannot afford the money required to join expensive treatment programmes or go into therapy for a year or two. Regard me as your therapist and this book as going to therapy. The book contains all the same interventions for sexually addictive behaviour that can be found in our group programme at the Marylebone Centre for Psychological Therapies or in individual therapy. It is divided into the same sequence of subjects that we use in our treatment programme. The only difference is that you will have to read it and do the exercises in your private time. At the end of this chapter, I will outline some suggestions that might be helpful to break the isolation and provide you with support and accountability. Addiction is a disease of disconnectedness, and connectedness is crucial to change and transformation.

Using this book

This book is a recovery tool, rather than just a book to read. It is an instruction manual for DIY recovery and should be treated like a guidebook. It is a step-by-step guide, designed to help you change your behaviour, based upon a 10-week recovery programme.

This first section of the book contains six readings, which need to be digested and understood before you begin the 10-week programme. You can read them all at once or space them according to your available time. However, they are not just a light read and it is important to understand the content of each of them. You might want to read each of them more than once. The six chapters focus upon the following topics: cognitive behavioural therapy, sexual addiction, supernormal stimuli, shame, neuroscience and attachment. The chapter on cognitive behavioural therapy outlines the main therapeutic approach upon which this book is based. It is important to understand this therapeutic model, as it will form the basis of your recovery work. The next chapter is a review of the concept of sexual addiction and a little about the history of the concept. It will help you to decide whether you are actually a sex addict. The concept of 'supernormal stimuli' is then explained with its relevance to the use of the internet as compulsive sexual behaviour. In the following chapter, shame is defined and explained in detail. There is then a long section on the neuroscience that lies behind sexual addiction. This is to help you see that the behaviour is not just about making wrong choices. It helps to explain why wrong choices seem to be so regularly made. The readings end with an explanation of 'attachment styles'. These are early patterns set up by our relationship with our caregivers and tend to operate throughout the life span.

Once these readings have been digested, you will be in a position to start the 10-week recovery programme, which is set out in Part II of the book. Each chapter of the recovery programme is designed to be done in a week. You do not have to stick to that timetable. You may want to spend more time on one section than another. You might want to repeat some of the sections. You are free to work at a pace that suits you. The topics covered are as follows:

Week 1: Core Belief and Formulation
Week 2: Values Clarification
Week 3: Harmful Consequences and Worst Case Scenario
Week 4: Provisional Sex Plan
Week 5: Family of Origin
Week 6: Cycle of Addiction
Week 7: Exiting the Cycle
Week 8: Cognitive Distortions
Week 9: Personal History
Week 10: Relapse Prevention

Many of these terms will probably be unfamiliar to you at this stage, but there will be a step-by-step explanation of them throughout the book. Each week includes background information about the topic, as well as exercises for you to undertake to help you understand and change your own addictive patterns. You should set aside a certain amount of time each week for these exercises and turn your attention to the task in hand. It might be a good idea to write a note in your diary, perhaps allowing a slot of two hours at the same time each week. One or two of the exercises take more time. You should do your recovery work in a quiet space where interruptions are minimal. In addition to undertaking the written exercises, you might find it helpful to make use of the space provided at the end of each chapter to write notes about your own personal learning.

Each week of the programme also includes a 'pillar'. The pillars are helpful devices to further your immersion in the process of recovery; they consist of some phrases for you to repeat to yourself on a regular basis. There is an introductory pillar at the end of this chapter, followed by 10 more pillars which you will find at the end of each of the chapters that comprise the recovery programme. I would suggest that you read the pillar given in each chapter three times a day during that week of the programme: once in the morning, once during the day and finally, out loud before you go to bed. The purpose of this repetitious behaviour is to create 'neurogenesis'. Each time you read the pillar, it creates an effect in the brain that keeps you in recovery mode and reinforces a commitment to recovery. You can go back and reread pillars that you have used before and found particularly helpful. However, I would suggest that you avoid reading them all at once or rushing on ahead to read them.

In Part III of the workbook there are four ancillary readings, designed to expand your knowledge and understanding of sexual addiction. The first chapter is on the internet and sexually compulsive behaviour. This is followed by a chapter on quirky sexual patterns and another on some of the problems that can accompany sexual addiction. Finally, there is an outline of available groups and places to connect with others wrestling with the same problem. The book finishes with a resource list of books and organisations that can help you with your ongoing recovery.

A word about ambivalence

At this stage, we should consider ambivalence. We are all ambivalent about giving up an addictive substance or an addictive activity. After all, why would you want to give up something that is so exciting and offers such a reward? The answer to that lies in the consequences of the behaviour. In advance, it seems unstoppable but afterwards you probably ask yourself 'Why did I do it again?' You have probably become sharply aware of the negative consequences that would occur if you were found out. You might realise that the behaviour is a threat to your relationship. With sexual addiction, the desire to stop comes and goes, depending on where you are in the addictive cycle. There will be more about the cycle of addiction in a later section of this book, but for now it is important to understand that ambivalence follows the cycle: the nearer you are to 'acting out' (the term that we use to describe engaging in compulsive sexual behaviour), the less committed you are to stopping, and afterwards, the less time that has passed since acting out, the greater the resolve. So the resolve to stop increases immediately after acting out and then fades as you make your way through the cycle towards the next episode of acting out. Ambivalence is a natural component of addiction. Just accept it.

Developing the reflective self

You will need to develop an astute 'reflective self' if you are going to change the behaviour and leave behind unwanted sexual behaviour. The reflective self is the part of the self that can observe the rest of the self. It is from this observation that change can be made. This book is designed to give you exercises that will help develop the reflective self. Take, for example, a patient of mine with panic attacks and overwhelming self-absorption. When we are in therapy, I can see him begin to descend into a bad place as he tells me how bad things have been. His constant rumination on feeling bad, and how bad he has felt, lowers his feeling states further. When I ask him about the future, he brightens up and his mood lifts. There is clearly a direct relationship between what he is thinking about and his mood states. I have pointed this out and he has seen the point. The more time he spends on worrying about feeling bad, the worse it becomes. The more time he spends planning and visualising the future, the more optimistic he feels. My task was to bring this to his attention. Using the reflective self, the part of the self that can stand outside the self and see the self, could have brought him independently to that conclusion. So your task is to get good at understanding yourself and seeing and understanding your patterns of behaviour. Figure 1.1.1 illustrates how this works. As you will see in the next chapter, this is the single most important feature of cognitive behavioural therapy: we can change our behaviour by observing ourselves and thinking differently, and applying the insight gained from this process of self-analysis to our future behaviours.

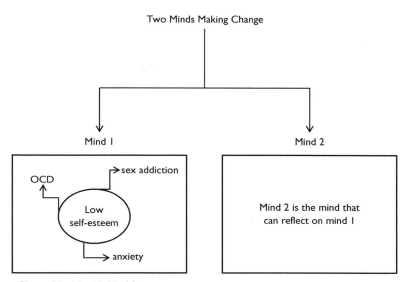

Change Mind I with Mind 2
1. by increased awareness
2. by involvement in a relationship that partially reparents
3. application of CBT tools to the problem

Figure 1.1.1 Reflective self.

Immersion

Part of the work that needs to be done in recovering from sex addiction is the process of immersion. Rather than immersing yourself in internet pornography or in the pursuit of sex workers, you have to immerse yourself in a culture of recovery. You become what you spend your time doing: if you run you become slim, if you study you become an expert, if you dance you become a dancer, and if you practise the piano you become a piano player. Whatever you practise, over time, you get good at. Practice is just the laborious repetition of an action until it becomes automatic. The exercises provided in this book are aimed at helping you learn to make alternative choices to sexual acting out. The more you practise, the easier it becomes and the better you get at it. It is difficult at first and there are many mistakes but, if you keep at it, things will change. If you are willing to go to any length, you will get the results.

This is where reading is important. Reading is like an internal conversation with another person. We become changed by what we read and by the things that absorb us. Immerse yourself in a culture of recovery and even the immersion process will start to make changes in your thinking and in your insights. If you would like some additional reading material on the subjects covered in this book, you might obtain a copy of Patrick Carnes' book *Out of the Shadows* or Paula Hall's book *Understanding and Treating Sexual Addiction*. These are two excellent introductory texts on the subject of sexual addiction and will provide you with helpful insights. You could also get my book *CBT for Compulsive Sexual Behaviour – A Guide for Professionals*. Although meant primarily for professionals working with men with sexually compulsive behaviours, it contains a great deal of useful information. This book, *Overcoming Sexual Addiction*, draws on all the information given in the first book and sets it out in a self-help style. You can also browse through the reading lists produced by the major distributors of books and look up sexual addiction. See if there is anything on the lists that appeals to you or resonates with your situation. You can also go to the Resources section at the end of this book for helpful ideas.

So begin to try and sink yourself into recovery from compulsive sexual behaviour, through reading, through doing the exercise programme in this book and, just maybe, by joining a group or going along to one of the recovery fellowships.

Getting connected

This book is meant for those who do not have any other recovery resource; however, that does not mean that you are entirely on your own. At least, you do not have to be entirely alone. As we all know, it is difficult for one lump of coal to burn by itself; it usually needs a couple of others to start a fire. You already have me and you, or, at least, this book and you. There are other possibilities, such as joining a group. We run groups at the Marylebone Centre, which are attended by a range of people from across the spectrum, including barristers, policemen, solicitors, teachers, students, sportsmen and clergy.

Another possibility is to join a Twelve Step programme. I will write more about these later in this book; they meet almost everywhere in the United Kingdom and they can provide important company on the journey. Have a look at the websites for Sex Addicts Anonymous or Sex and Love Addicts Anonymous and see if there are meetings near enough for you to get to easily. These are just non-professional groups of men and women who are sexually addicted and who come together for mutual support and encouragement. You could always go along to one of these meetings. You do not have to say anything and you could just take it in. You would probably need to go to several meetings before making a decision about whether or not it might be a way to break your isolation in the problem. There are also online meetings of these groups and it might be possible to find an online sponsor. A sponsor is someone in recovery who has a bit more experience in overcoming sexual addiction and you could enlist this person as your support person.

Another idea would be to choose a couple of trusted friends and tell them that you are setting out on a recovery journey. You would have to explain the nature of the problem and ask them if they would be willing to help you along. I would suggest, if this is feasible, that you might ask them whether they would be willing to meet with you about once a month for an hour or so to review your progress. You might feel too much shame about the behaviour to do this, but shame is diminished when it is spoken about to non-judgemental others. If they are your friends, I think that they might well feel complimented to be asked to help you in this way. It tells them that you trust them.

Another idea is to find an accountability partner. This is much the same idea as above but would involve one individual who you trust and to whom you could explain the situation. If you go down this route, I would suggest that you have a meeting with them once a week. This could be face-to-face or it could be by telephone or email. If the problem is internet addiction, there are programmes that will email your internet searches to an accountability partner. The programme 'Covenant Eyes', for example, will send a record of your internet usage to a designated third party. This is a good way to prevent your misuse of the internet.

Another way to create some help with this process is to approach your pastor, priest or other religious leader. You could tell them about the problem and ask if they would be your accountability partner. It also probably makes sense to interview them in advance to see whether you think the person might be on your wavelength. I think you might time-limit it to 3–6 months so that the commitment is not forever.

In any case, no matter what alternative you adopt, suggest that you try it out provisionally for six weeks so that you can see how it is going. Do not be afraid to fire an accountability partner if they are not giving you what you need for your recovery. You will know if they are helping or not. Do not be too hasty in making a decision, so that you can be sure that it is the right decision.

Finally, you could go into therapy. There are a lot of therapists about, although most are not experienced in working with sexual addiction. They would want to help. If you choose this option, simply tell them what you have in mind and, if they agree, then set it in motion as above. Keep in mind that it needs a trial period. A lot of therapists work from home so it need not cost a fortune. You could see if they would agree to meet with you monthly. The thing about therapists is that you can guarantee their confidentiality. They would lose their professional accreditation if they were to break confidentiality. Recent studies (Schmitz 2005) show that psychotherapy can make changes to the brain chemistry of the patient. Hudson-Allez (2009) writes that the therapeutic process can make good the deficits that we have inherited from our history. In other words, we tend to become like those with whom we spend time. We unconsciously internalise the other. This is an important function of psychotherapy. We unconsciously internalise the therapist. This generally means internalising self-acceptance, compassion and the absence of judgement. So, I am recommending that you might consider getting into therapy. One of the things that I have found to be true about recovery is this rule of thumb: the things that you want to do least are the things that you should do most of all.

If your sexual behaviours are verging on the illegal, you would need to approach therapy with great care. While independent practitioners are not required to disclose illegal activity, some would feel an ethical responsibility to do this, so check with them in advance about their personal policy on disclosure. Unfortunately, this can put people in a no-win situation: disclosure is important to get help to stop the problem but, at the same time, disclosure may not be allowed and the problem remains unresolved.

Concluding words

The aim of cognitive behavioural therapy (CBT) – the therapeutic approach used in this book – is to turn the patient into the therapist. This means imparting information and insight that will become the basis for a permanent change in behaviour. The goal of reading this book and doing the exercises in it is to gain insight and learn to apply it to your specific situation. This is the same process that takes place within cognitive behavioural therapy; the only difference is that I am a distant therapist and the process is not one of interactive minute-by-minute exchange but one where I present the information and provide the exercises that will, hopefully, take you to a place of greater understanding and behavioural change.

You are an addict and addicts are used to instant change. You will be tempted to do everything at once. That is not a good idea. How long did it take for you to become an addict? How long have you been using sex to anaesthetise unruly feeling states? The reality is that, if you have been using sexual behaviour as a mood modifying behaviour for a long time, recovery will not come instantly. You need to realise that this is a much slower process. It involves a lot of work. Quick fixes and instant answers are simply not available. I wish it were not so but, alas, it is. Try to get used to the idea that this is a gentle process but one that needs sustained application and a great resolve. It will not go forward perfectly and there will be lapses. You might already be thinking about acting out and looking forward to getting onto the internet and looking at some porn. Even the anxiety caused by trying to fix the problem can trigger an urge to act out. Not to worry, it will all become clear. You can now get started. I wish you well on the journey. It is a journey that can take you from shame to grace. I hope you experience that in working through this book.

Introductory pillar

This pillar is to be recited three times a day while you are reading the preliminary readings. The last time you read it each day, it should be read out loud.

I am going to change. I have lived too long with sexually compulsive behaviour. At first, these sexual things just happened but eventually they hardened into a compulsion. This compulsion has controlled my life for too long. Now it is the time for change. Addiction has affected almost everything about me. It has shaped my thoughts, driven my desires, taken time from my diary, affected my relationships and blighted my life. Most importantly, addiction has reduced my capacity for relationships and has seriously hurt the ones I love. But now, I am going to change. This is my resolve and my commitment. I will change. I can do it. I know that I can make the changes that are necessary. I will commit to the programme outlined in this book. More importantly, addiction recovery will become my top priority. I will change. I know that I can do it. I will change.

Chapter 2

Cognitive behavioural therapy

As this is a cognitive behavioural therapy (CBT) self-help book, our first task will be to ensure that we understand the basic components of CBT. Cognitive behavioural therapy emerged in the 1970s and can be seen as a real revolution in the behavioural and cognitive sciences. It represents a significant break from traditional psychotherapies, like the psychoanalysis of Freud or Jung. The 'grandfather' of CBT, Albert Ellis, was a psychoanalyst by training, but noticed that his clients were not benefitting from traditional therapeutic approaches like accessing their unconscious, but instead were achieving progress by changing the way that they saw themselves and their environment. It was then Aaron Beck who recognised that mood disorders were primarily 'thinking disorders'. Both he and Ellis realised that psychological distress is not caused by what happens to us, but rather by how we think about and interpret our experiences. They argued that the way in which we think about ourselves, others and the world significantly impacts upon the way we feel and the way we behave. When we experience psychological distress, our thinking becomes more rigid and distorted, and our beliefs about ourselves, others and the world become increasingly fixed. Faulty thinking processes lead to negative emotions, which result in self-defeating behaviour patterns, leading to more faulty thinking and creating a vicious circle.

In CBT, change occurs when the client understands the link between his thoughts, feelings and behaviour and can challenge and correct any unhelpful thinking patterns. The role of the CBT therapist is primarily to help the client to identify and change these maladaptive thought patterns, which will in turn lead to changes in feelings and changes in behaviour. CBT therapists often also make use of behavioural techniques to help patients achieve positive changes in their lives. They act in many ways as guides or teachers, helping the client to develop new understanding and new ways of thinking.

So, the major insight of CBT is that it is not external events that determine our feelings, but rather it is our *interpretation* of the events that
creates our feeling states. In other words, our feelings follow on from our
thoughts about the events. Let us look at a few examples.

Aaron was arrested for voyeurism shortly before taking his final exams
in a discipline related to medicine. This arrest meant that he could no
longer pursue a career in medicine. This would be a sad day for many
people, but for him it was a happy release. He never really wanted to study
medicine in the first place. It was family pressure that was pushing him
into it. It was his interpretation of the event that meant that this was not
experienced as a tragedy but rather as a release from the obligations of the
family.

The lease on Tom's flat was not renewed. He did not rue the day
because this allowed him to move out of London into a much greener
environment. The end of the lease, which many would interpret as a source
of distress, was, for Tom, a matter of hope.

Even death itself is not a matter of distress; it all depends on how we
interpret it. For William, death was not the end, but rather the beginning of
a new venture into a glorious eternity.

So, it is not the event that matters and generates our feelings, but rather
our interpretation of the event. This is equally true with sexual addiction.
The principal and crucial definition of sexual addiction is that it is a pattern
of behaviour that generates subjective distress and contributes to the loss
of important professional, recreational and domestic opportunities. In other
words, people are involved in a repeating set of sexual activities that cause
them distress and despair. If your use of sex workers is not a problem to
you, does not interfere with your life goals, does not create financial ruin
and does not upset your relationship, then what is the problem? There
might be moral judgements brought by others but these judgements are
their view and you are free to agree with them or not. As I say over and
over, 'it is only a problem, if it is a problem'. The majority of men who are
involved in our treatment programme come in order to protect an important
relationship with a much-loved partner. The value of the relationship and
of their family life has overriding significance.

Another insight from CBT is that our behaviour has an important influence on our thoughts and feelings. We normally think of it the other way
round, believing that our thoughts and feelings generate our behaviours.
However, both are true: our behaviours influence our thoughts and feelings,
as well as our feelings and thoughts generating our behaviour. We might act
out sexually because we feel anxious. However, if we change our behaviour
and do not act out, this will change our feelings and our thoughts. This is an

example of behaviour affecting thoughts and feelings. Similarly, if I go for a run when I do not feel like it, afterwards I have good feelings of competency and self-control. If I actually go on a diet and forswear my taste for too much good food, I might have to exercise some willpower, but in the end I will feel much better and more effective, with a sense of self-mastery. People who have undertaken an abstinence contract (deciding not to be sexual at all) for a period of time report that they feel much better and more optimistic, as well as more in control. All the men in our sexual recovery groups report feeling better and happier once their sexual behaviour is under control. So it is a two-way street: thoughts and feelings give rise to behaviours but behaviours also give rise to feelings and thoughts.

CBT tends to understand things not as a dichotomy between order and disorder but rather as problems and issues somewhere on a continuum. Take depression, for instance: it is on a continuum from 'not at all' to 'I can't get out of bed'. All of us are somewhere on this scale between perfectly well, to a little depressed, to more depressed, to very depressed. When does it become a disorder? I think the answer to that is when the person concerned feels that it is a problem and wants to change the situation. When is sexual behaviour problematic? The answer to that is when the behaviour is deemed to be unacceptable to the person concerned. In other words, when the downside of the behaviour becomes so great that the person really feels that it has to stop so that other important values and lifestyle choices can come to the fore. Sexual addiction is, for some, simply an exaggeration of otherwise normal behaviour.

Another feature of CBT is that it sees things as parts of an interconnected system. This system is normally made up of thoughts, feelings, behaviours and physiological responses. Figure 1.2.1 shows how this works. We sometimes refer to this as the 'hot cross bun' diagram because of its shape. Notice that thoughts are at the top of the system, reflecting the CBT insight that feelings flow from thought and that behaviours and physiological responses flow from feelings.

Here is an example: David acts out on anxiety and shame. He has an important deadline ahead of him, a contract negotiation (thought), that causes him anxiety and fear (feeling). This becomes intolerable and he needs an escape. Sexual behaviour is his normal escape route. The anxiety about the deadline gives rise to bodily discomfort and he experiences an increased heart rate and sweaty palms. These change to feelings of sexual excitement as he begins the process of sexual involvement. The interconnection between all these factors is shown in Figure 1.2.2.

Let's take another example: Roger 'acts out' on loneliness. He has a weekend ahead of him with nothing much to do and no one to do it with.

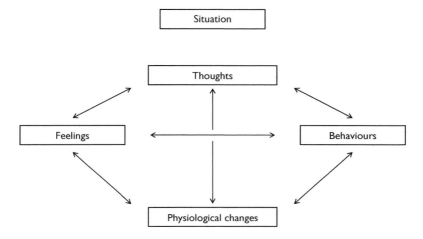

Figure 1.2.1 Hot cross bun diagram.
Source: Adapted from Padesky and Mooney 1990.

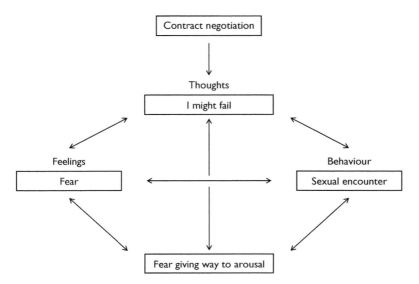

Figure 1.2.2 Contract negotiation.

He thinks, 'I am alone'. Focusing on being alone creates intolerable feelings of loneliness. His thoughts turn to sexual acting out as an escape from loneliness. He acts out sexually. There are other ways to solve the problem of loneliness. He could meet a friend, go to a social club or take up an interactive activity, such as playing bridge or learning how to dance. These solutions might actually solve the problem of loneliness. Roger, however, who is predisposed to sexual acting out, will act out alone on the internet. The use of the internet is a solitary occupation and further loneliness ensues.

Exercise: the urge diary

Generally, sexual compulsive behaviours do not fall out of the sky, but rather they emerge from the negative feeling states that precede them. It is important to be able to notice and monitor these feelings and behaviours. In order to do this, you can use an 'urge diary' (see Table 1.2.1), which is a written record of your urges to act out. Every time you have an urge to act out, record it and make a note of what exactly was going on just before the urge. This will help you to see that there are specific triggers for your acting out. Sometimes you might find that there are particular people that prompt the urge, while at other times you might find certain environments trigger the urge, as well as certain unwelcome feeling states. For example, you might notice that your thoughts turn to acting out when you are bored, or maybe anxious or lonely. It is important to notice these feeling states and eventually to learn other ways to manage them.

Once you have noted what was going on that prompted the urge, go on to note down the strength of the urge, on a scale of 1 to 10, and how long it persisted. Record whether or not you acted on the urge, and if so, what you did and how long it lasted. Then note down how you felt afterwards. If you can, see whether you can identify any alternative behaviours that you could have pursued instead of acting out. This process of thinking about alternative behaviours will become important in the overall journey into full recovery.

Remember, it is not the urge that is important but the circumstances that generated the urge. Once you are able to identify a context for the urge, you will be able to generate an alternative to compulsive sexual behaviour. The new strategy will not give so much immediate gratification but it will give you much better long-term results.

For example, you might be sitting at your desk, bored and unwilling to actually do the slog required for the afternoon. The idea will come into your mind to have a look at an erotic website. You might think that this

Table 1.2.1 Urge diary

Date/time	What was going on prior? Examples: alcohol, loneliness, anxiety, stress, self-soothing	Strength of urge (1–10)	Time it persisted	Acted out? (Y/N)	If yes, how long and type. Examples: internet, webcams, anonymous sex	Feelings afterwards. Examples: shame, regret, self-attack, sadness	Alternative behaviours that could be or were used

has just popped into your mind, but the context is all important. Once you become aware that the sexual thoughts are a response to boredom and anxiety, you can circumvent the sexual by adopting a more effective long-term strategy.

The urge diary can act as a record of progress as you go through this self-help treatment programme. It will give you important information that will be useful in attempting to move out of sexual addiction and into a more balanced way of life. I would suggest that you start the urge diary this week and keep it for the full 10 weeks that you use this self-help pro-gramme. You can photocopy the urge diary from the table (it is free to photocopy for your personal use) or just copy it out by hand. It is probably not a good idea to leave it lying around for others to see. I would suggest that you keep the diary with you at all times. Some people prefer to organise it on their computer or telephone. The important thing is that you complete it as near to the event as possible. If you leave it, you are likely to forget it or not remember it accurately.

See if you are able to reduce the acting out response to the urge during this recovery programme. It might be helpful to have a look at the diary from week to week. You might get an increase in urges in the first week or two, just caused by the anxiety that is created by trying to do something about your sexual addiction. Even just thinking about not doing it can trigger thoughts about doing it. So, take care and see how you progress.

Summarise what you have learned about cognitive behavioural therapy:

_____

_____

_____

_____

_____

_____

_____

_____

_____

_____

Chapter 3

Sexual addiction

This chapter will explore the concept of sexual addiction, but let us start with what sexual addiction is not. It is not about a high sex drive or about liking a lot of sex. It is not about the kind of sex that you like or what you want to do alone or with another person. Nor is it about your sexual fantasy life or what you think about or look at when you masturbate. Sex is a normal human need and a persistent human longing; that is why we call it a 'drive' instead of merely an option. In the human species, there is considerable variation across a wide spectrum of possible sexual alternatives, from straightforward heterosexual vaginal intercourse, and all the possible variations involved in that, to same-sex behaviour with all of its possible variations. Sexual addiction is not about same-sex behaviours or a preference for solitary behaviours. Nor is it about preferences for group sex, bondage, dominance and submission, or anything else some might describe as unusual. This book is not about *not* having sex. It is about having good sex that you can enjoy and feel good about after you have done it.

The concept of sexual addiction goes back a long way. In the third century, Augustine wrote about addiction (and was probably referring to sexual behaviour) without using the term 'addiction'. He wrote as follows:

> The enemy had my power of willing in his clutches, and from it had forged a chain to bind me. The truth is that disordered lust springs for a perverted will; when lust is pandered to, a habit is formed; and when the pattern is not checked, it hardens into a compulsion. These were the interlinking rings forming what I have described as a chain, and my harsh servitude used it to keep me under duress.
>
> (Augustine, translated by Boulding 1997: 192)

A long time later, Patrick Carnes (1983) developed and promoted the concept of sexual addiction in his book *Out of the Shadows*. This book has been the inspiration and the foundation of all recent work on sexual addiction.

Sexual addiction is said to be a pattern of behaviour that has four components: it feels out of control, it brings harmful consequences, it is seemingly impossible to stay stopped from and it has a function. The first three characteristics apply to all sexual behaviour. Good sex involves a loss of control. It is the loss of self into erotic oblivion. Sex usually has consequences, some good and some bad. It is hard to stay stopped because sex is a fundamental human drive. The big factor that lies behind sex addiction is that it is not about sex; rather, it is a learned way of escaping and avoiding negative feeling states. So sexual addiction is distinctive in that it is the use of sexual behaviour to anaesthetise a negative feeling state. However, it can be difficult to tell whether you are responding to an inner biological drive or whether you are just bored and want some excitement.

You might have your suspicions that you are a sex addict. It is probably the reason you bought this book. Your partner may have suspicions because the book was bought for you. However, you are the only one who can tell if your sexual patterns are actually compulsive. To help answer this question, we can go to Carnes. He gives us Ten Signs of Sexual Addiction:

1   A pattern of out-of-control behaviour.
2   Severe consequences due to sexual behaviour.
3   Inability to stop despite adverse consequences.
4   Persistent pursuit of self-destructive or high-risk behaviour.
5   Ongoing desire or effort to limit sexual behaviour.
6   Sexual obsession and fantasy as a primary coping strategy.
7   Increasing amounts of sexual experience because the current level of activity is no longer sufficient.
8   Severe mood changes around sexual activity.
9   Inordinate amounts of time spent in obtaining sex, being sexual or recovering from sexual experience.
10 Neglect of important social, occupational or recreational activities because of sexual behaviour.

(Carnes 1991: 11–12)

According to Carnes, 'sex addicts use their sexuality as a medication for sleep, anxiety, pain and family and life problems' (1991: 23). Having read through the 10 signs, ask yourself whether you can say yes to many or all of them. For example, perhaps you realise that your sexual patterns are disrupting your relationship with your partner or that you keep getting into work late because you have been up during the night watching internet pornography. Maybe you have missed something important or your relationship is under threat because of your use of sex workers.

The core of sexual addiction really lies in the way you feel about yourself deep down. Baumeister writes that addiction is an 'escape from the self' (Baumeister 1991: 21). He writes that, when you do not feel good about yourself, you have a need to escape the negative feeling states and move into pleasurable oblivion. Sexual addiction is the repeated use of sexual behaviour to escape intolerable feeling states. You may think that you feel good about yourself because you have made money, or won academic awards or been promoted at work, but these are sometimes defences against the true feelings of 'not being enough'. Underneath these defences, often even unrecognised by the self, is a sense that one is not measuring up.

I had a patient who was a lawyer. He was the last son of a family of seven sons. He was intelligent, good looking and successful at work. He had the capacity to write a blockbuster of a novel but this was never fulfilled. He spent every evening sitting at home watching pornography. If the same amount of time and energy had been put into something different, he could have achieved a sort of greatness but it was all wasted on the internet. He had nothing to show for these endless hours. They were just escapes into oblivion. Now, maybe, we all sometimes need to escape into oblivion but, in this case, night after night was given over to the same unproductive process. He had little to show for the years he had spent trying to escape his inner sense of not being enough. If instead he had written the book, he would have something to show for it and the success of a book would have heightened his sense of self-worth and abrogated his sense of not being enough. Sexual addiction is never a solution to low self-esteem; in fact, it contributes to low self-esteem. Productive activity does the reverse; it builds and solidifies higher levels of self-worth.

Maybe you are at school or university and are working towards a degree. Time spent studying will take you forward to the degree. Lots of time spent looking at the internet will waste your time and lower your possibilities for the future. Sexual addiction is about short-term gain and long-term loss. Better to bite the bullet and study hard than to escape the tedium of study through the internet.

Low self-worth is sometimes accompanied by low self-care. It works like this: you think you are not worth much and therefore you do not look after yourself. You wear any old thing. You do not make sure that your clothes are ironed. You postpone going to the dentist or the optician. You do not eat properly. You drink too much. You do not take regular exercise.

This accumulates and converts into further neglect and this, too, contributes to the need to escape into oblivion. The oblivion might be alcohol, recreational drugs and/or internet pornography.

Sometimes people just move into the use of internet pornography by finding themselves in difficult situations that they find hard to manage. Perhaps you feel like a loner and that everyone else is going out with others and you are not doing the same. Over and over, in working with sex addicts, I find that there is often an escalation in the use of the internet or the use of sex workers during times of crisis. It can be seemingly insoluble problems with the partner, or her pregnancy or even the partner being ill and in hospital. The worry is too great to bear and there is an escape to be found in strip clubs or on the internet. You are not setting out to be unfaithful, you are just trying to manage the anxiety by escaping into oblivion.

The word addiction comes from the Latin *addicare* which means 'bound over by judicial decree'. It represents the loss of freedom. Think again about Augustine's words: 'a compulsion ... interlinking rings forming a chain'. At the beginning of one recovery group, a man cried out 'I just want to be free'. The purpose of the book is to help you to be free.

Summarise what you have learned about sexual addiction:

_____

_____

_____

_____

_____

_____

_____

_____

_____

Chapter 4

Supernormal stimuli

A large number of men who come into our clinic for treatment are addicted to internet pornography. This is not about occasional use but rather an extensive and time-involved pattern. The sense of self is lost in sexual behaviour. For these men, this loss of self can go on for hours and even days. I can think of two men who would spend the best part of two days a week, for several years, masturbating to internet pornography. In order to understand the particularly strong allure of internet pornography, we need to turn to the concept of 'supernormal stimuli'.

Let's imagine that I have just had dinner and I am presented with a choice: I can have a real orange or I can have a chocolate orange. Unless I have great self-discipline, I will go for the chocolate orange. In other words, I prefer the unreal to the real. I prefer the artificially enhanced, extra-sweet product, filled with artificial sweeteners and fake flavours over the reality of the natural orange. This same analysis could be applied to sex. When you are given the choice between a real naked woman and an artificially enhanced naked woman, you might well choose the artificially enhanced. This is the basis of pornography. Pornography is the presentation of the exaggerated over the real; the artificially enhanced images become more alluring than the reality of the real woman. The chocolate orange and the woman on the screen are both examples of 'supernormal stimuli', in other words artificial exaggerations of the real thing.

To understand the role of supernormal phenomena in sexual addiction, we need to understand the work of the Nobel Prize winner, Niko Tinbergen. He was a Dutch naturalist with a particular interest in the observation of birds and mammals. He left the Netherlands after the war and went to teach at Merton College, Oxford. He studied the stickleback, the most common fish in Dutch waters, and discovered that they would respond to exaggerated models of the real stickleback. The dummies that he used could surpass the power of the real thing. He found similar patterns with geese; they would prefer to sit on exaggerated fake eggs to natural ones. He also studied birds that lay small pale blue eggs and found that females preferred to sit on unreal eggs that were bright blue with polka dots. Tinbergen concluded from these studies that an artificially enhanced stimulus can be more powerful than the real thing, and it was he who named these artificially enhanced stimuli 'supernormal stimuli' (Barrett 2010).

Another example can be taken from Dr Deidre Barratt (2010), a psychologist who teaches at Harvard Medical School, and who studied the artificial enhancement of barn swallows. Male barn swallows have light brown chests and females choose the ones with the most intense colour as an indication of fitness. Scientists with a $5.99 felt-tip marker darkened the chest of a scorned male and suddenly the females lined up to mate with him (Barrett 2010).

All of these examples help to point us to an understanding of the role of supernormal phenomena in human sexual behaviour. Dr Donald Hilton, a neurosurgeon at the University of Texas, writes 'with plastic surgery enhanced breasts serving the same purpose as artificially enhanced female butterflies ... the males of each species prefer the artificial to the naturally evolved' (Hilton 2013: 5).

Eoin Stephens, President of the PCI College (Personal Counselling Institute) in Dublin, writes that supernormal stimuli are artificially enhanced stimuli, which create responses in our thinking, our emotions, our physiological reactions and behaviour that are hard to resist (Stephens 2012). They do this by subverting and hijacking evolved appetitive instincts and motivational systems and by over-stimulating their associated neural pathways.

Hilton, writing about pornography, makes the point that this addictive effect 'may be amplified by the accelerated novelty and the supranormal stimulus factor afforded by Internet pornography' (Hilton 2013: 1). Human beings are novelty-seeking creatures. There is ample novelty in the 400 million pages of internet pornography (Maltz and Maltz 2008).

Naomi Wolf writes, 'Today, real naked women are just bad porn' (Wolf no date). Maltz and Maltz (2008: 35) quote some interesting statistics from *Men's Health* magazine, March 2004 and *The Smart Girls Guide to Porn*: the average length of a man's erect penis is 5.8 inches, while the average length of a male porn star's erect penis is 8 inches; moreover, 85 per cent of female porn stars have breast implants. Here we see supernormal stimuli illustrated very well from the world of pornography.

In a Question and Answer article in *The Harvard Crimson*, Hilton said this of internet pornography: 'When we orgasm, we release a neurotransmitter called oxytocin which causes bonding, so we are literally bonding to porn when we get off – making breaking the addiction that much harder'

(*The Harvard Crimson* 2011). If this is true, the same would apply to the creation of addiction in the use of sex workers and the use of other sexual outlets. When we orgasm with, or to, an exaggeration of the real thing, we are creating a biologically determined bond to an exaggerated stimulus. This may account for the persistence of certain arousal cues that come with people, places and fetish objects. We come to prefer the exaggeration to the naturally evolved. Excitement about the artificially enhanced is greater than the excitement of the reality of the woman. It is similar with sex workers; they may exude a kind of femaleness that a partner of 20 or 30 years cannot equal. The stimulus provided by these substitutes attenuates the attractiveness of the ordinary woman. Men with pornography addiction often withdraw sexually from their partners. The supernormal stimulus is preferred over the reality of the woman. Naomi Wolf, author of eight books including *The Vagina: A Biography*, writing in the *New York* magazine, states that, 'In the end, porn doesn't whet men's appetites, it turns them off of the real thing' (Wolf no date). She continues, 'The onslaught of porn is responsible for deadening male libido in relation to real women … leading men to see fewer and fewer women as porn worthy' (Wolf no date). This is the effect of supernormal stimuli. Perhaps this is why so many men presenting at our clinic with an addiction to internet pornography have difficulty sustaining sex with a real partner.

Pornography is made for men. Yes, there is specially made pornography for women but the use of pornography is almost exclusively a male preoccupation. Male sexuality is visual. There is a preoccupation with parts of the body and items of dress that enhance or reveal the female figure. The natural order in our species is that women attract and men are attracted. The capacity for men to notice reproductive capability and the capacity of women to advertise reproductive capability is crucial for the continuation of the species. Those who notice better, and those who advertise better, have a better chance of propagation. These seem to me to be instinctual processes that are biologically mandated.

On the internet, the sexual genre that we prefer matches our predetermined sexual template. Some men with exhibitionist tendencies will prefer mock exhibitionist pornography. Other men, more interested in the 'build up' to sexual behaviour, will spend their time accessing sex worker sites, researching and planning or fantasising about sexual contact. One gay patient who was interested in fat men would spend hours searching the internet to see sexual pictures of fat, older men involved in sexual activity.

We have mirror neurons in our brains that allow us to resonate with the feeling states of other people when we are given visual cues. When we do not get the visual cues, it is hard to feel the feelings of another. I was working with a woman who had been sexually abused by her stepfather. Her appearance was one of utter tranquillity and serenity as she told me the story of her abuse. For this reason, I could not feel, in myself, any of the horror or disgust she was feeling. I was feeling serene because she was looking serene. The mirror neurons allow us to feel what the other is feeling. Much of this is visual; less is in the actual content of the words that are used to describe situations. In terms of pornography, we can be aroused by the arousal of others. On the internet these arousal signals are amplified and exaggerated. The female characters are not just vocal during intercourse but make loud and exaggerated sounds of sexual pleasure. They are often in exaggerated sexual positions: large breasts showing, emphasised buttocks and painted lips. Nothing seems too much for them: vaginal, anal and oral penetration, and perhaps all three simultaneously. Normally they are accompanied by fetish clothing, such as high heels and stockings. They all seem to be keen on as much casual sex as possible and appear quite insatiable. Are real women really like this? I think not. These are exaggerations of the real thing and, as supernormal stimuli, the male can come to prefer them over the real thing. Spending half a lifetime looking at internet pornography can create a replacement for real women and set up unrealistic expectations in male viewers. This is a sexual manifestation of Tinbergen's artificial exaggeration becoming more attractive than the real thing. Looking at these sites would give a man the impression that he must be always be hard, always ejaculate and fully enjoy anal and oral sex, as well as vaginal sex. With real people, none of these things are necessarily true. The artificially enhanced can be more powerful than the real thing.

Summarise what you have learned about supernormal stimuli:

_____

_____

_____

_____

_____

_____

_____

_____

_____

_____

Chapter 5

Shame

Defining shame

Early memories of my own childhood come in snapshots and not in narratives. This is true for most of us. These snapshots are of both positive and negative experiences. My love of books and the adult creation of an enormous library clearly goes back to being taken to the library when I was three years old. I trace the start of my vocation as a priest to learning the Lord's Prayer and the 23rd Psalm when I was a child. I also trace and connect my experience of sexual shame to one particular childhood event: I was probably three years old and I was in the backyard with another child. I wanted to see his bottom. I was only interested in the curve of the buttock and I patted it gently. At that moment, my mother came on the scene, hysterical and furious. I learned then that I had done something terribly wrong and it has always stayed with me. This memory was like a branding. It was 36 years before I could even speak about it and every time I did, I had the awful feeling of shame arise within me. Even now, I still feel the anxiety of shame rise up inside of me, even though I know that I was doing nothing wrong and was involved in age-appropriate quasi-sexual exploration. But on this fateful day, sexual shame and body shame came together. I knew, and never forgot, that this part of me was bad. It is different today: I still feel it, but now I know that I did no wrong. My mother had implanted sexual shame within me. Before I came into recovery for sexual addiction, I thought it was authentic shame. Now when I feel it, I know this is just a 'shame script', in other words feelings of shame from my past, which, in reality, have no weight or validity. I have learned to say to myself, 'Here it comes, it is just a shame script. It has no validity.'

So, what is shame? It is an awful feeling arising from a belief that you are inherently and intrinsically defective. Shame is the sense that you are unlovable, deeply flawed, clumsy, stupid and, ultimately, that you have not made a mistake, but rather you *are* a mistake. It is a profoundly disturbing feeling state. Shame and guilt are both the same feeling state set up in the brain. The difference is that guilt represents a one-off transgression that can be remedied with an apology or the making of appropriate amends. Shame is an overall pervasive and toxic feeling that one is intrinsically flawed and it cannot be remedied. It is a watermark on the soul.

Shame had little place in the thinking and writing of scientists and researchers until recently. Subsequently psychotherapists, researchers, theologians and psychologists have begun to explore the nature of shame. In early recovery, I read *Healing the Shame that Binds You* by John Bradshaw (2005). I remember doing this on a cycling trip across France. This book created a revolution in my understanding of myself and the edifice of shame that had been constructed in my life. The nature of endemic shame has been laid out by many subsequent to Bradshaw, including family therapists, Fossum and Mason, who describe shame as follows:

> an inner state of being completely diminished or insufficient as a person. It is the self, judging the self ... a pervasive sense of shame is the ongoing experience that one is fundamentally bad, inadequate, defective, unworthy or not fully valid as a person.
>
> (Fossum and Mason 1986: 5)

Otto Will, a medical doctor in private practice in California, describes shame as a 'painful and unpleasant emotion' (Will 1987: 309). He writes that, to be ashamed is 'to be faced with censure and the possible removal of human support' (ibid.).

Shame reactions have distinctive characteristics that are similarly represented through all cultures. The body language of shame is universal. In other words, all people display shame in largely the same way. This includes the covered face, the averted gaze, the covered mouth, the bowed head and the body made smaller. Much can be told about the nature of shame in the reading of the body language: there is the need to hide and to make oneself invisible. The word 'shame' comes from the Indo-European word, *skem*, which means 'to hide'. As we know, 'hide' has two meanings. One is to put something where nobody can find it, while the other is the covering of, and container for, a person or an animal, as in 'rawhide', 'horsehide' and 'cowhide'. Shame suggests both of these meanings. It is a sense of self that is to be hidden and covered. The hide is also the defence against intrusion. And yet, shame does not even need the gaze of another. It can simply be the eye of the self, looking at the self.

So, shame brings with it a desire to hide and the requirement to cover up perceived inferiority. In my own case, my cover is made of the books and articles that I have written and the professional qualifications that I have gained. Another cover is just being nice to people. I work on the principle that if I have published enough, gained enough qualifications and am nice, then people will not notice that I am shameful. Others do the same thing. At a recovery group that I run, we had a session on the harmful consequences of sexual addiction. I was aware of how much 'being nice' was used to cover the deep-seated belief of 'I am defective'. For example, some members of the group smiled continuously when talking about painful matters and losses of great consequence.

We can learn about the nature of shame from the popular language used to describe it. People say that they were mortified, which technically means 'made dead'. Sometimes people will say 'I was so embarrassed that I wanted the ground to open up and swallow me'. One rabbi said, to me, in profoundly chilling language, 'I wanted to fly to the grave'. In all of these common terms to describe a shame experience, there is a reference to disappearance and death. Death is, after all, the final and complete disappearance.

Shame and sexual addiction

I am focusing in such great detail here on shame because there is a deep-seated link between shame and sexual addiction. Dr Donald Nathanson, a Clinical Professor of Psychiatry and a major contributor on the subject of shame, emphasises this connection. It is his view that the thoughts that come with sexual arousal are attempts to reverse shame. He notes that 'sexual fantasy is one of the ways we undo shame and reverse life experiences of shame at the hands of others' (Nathanson 1992: 286). Shame is the feeling state that emerges from the deep-seated belief that 'I am not worthy'. For sex addicts, sexual behaviour is the escape mechanism used to deaden and avoid the feelings of shame.

Another Professor of Psychiatry, the late Dr Robert Stoller, an important figure in psychoanalytic psychotherapy, studied sexuality and unusual forms of sexual behaviour. He concluded that sex is one of the ways that we 'undo shame and reverse the effect of humiliations, that striking from any direction, are defended against by each turn of the daydreams script' (Stoller 1987: 295).

In the novel *Rites of Passage* by William Golding (1980), a clergyman dies mysteriously of an unknown illness. It is only suggested in the last few pages of the book that he has died of shame. He had given oral sex to a sailor and eventually the shame was so great that he wasted to death. As we saw earlier, shame has about it intimations of death. I think this is because, in evolutionary terms, it would have meant abandonment. To be abandoned by the tribal horde would have threatened your existence. Similarly, if as a child you are abandoned by the family, you will not survive. The possibility that you will be abandoned by the group, the family or the partner all give rise to potential terror. Abandonment triggers fear about survival.

I am aware of how profoundly men are affected by the loss of a partner. Once their sexual addiction has been discovered, there is more than discomfort. There is a fear of effective annihilation. Without social support, the person is deconstructed. Studies on men and women in solitary confinement testify to this process. We are social creatures. Anything which might detach us from our fellows is much feared and anything that does detach us from the familiar hints of disintegration.

A patient of mine had been having a three-year affair with a woman he had met on a website. He had spent a great deal of money on her. He had made a lot of money in a business start-up. His own marriage was beset with problems. This woman sold her story to a tabloid newspaper for £20,000. One day in my office, my patient had a call from his wife. The journalists were outside their house. The wife knew nothing of the affair. I saw the most terrifying destruction. My patient went into a foetal position as his wife spoke to him on the phone. I will never forget seeing this tall, well-built man reduced to helplessness. Did that humiliation really serve the common good? This was simply destruction in the service of avarice.

Most people do not have shame at this volume and pitch, but almost all sex addicts have some shame. It is a multifaceted shame. Sexual addiction is usually driven by the desire to escape the painful feelings of shame. For most sex addicts, these feelings have their origin in childhood trauma. I am not suggesting that sex addicts were often sexually or physically abused (although some were) but most were raised in families that gave them the message that there was something wrong with them. I have a drawing by a man who had been shamed in childhood. The drawing was of a boy about 10 or 11 in a school uniform. There is a placard hung around his neck that reads, 'I am the problem' (see Figure 1.5.1). This belief came about as a result of having a constantly critical father and an unresponsive mother. The mother was so tied up in her own needs that the needs of her child became secondary. You, too, might have been the object of ridicule, brutality or other abusive behaviour. I think of Frank, whose father shoved his head into his dinner when he did not want to eat, or of Harry, whose father used to come into his room and smell his hands to find out whether he had

Figure 1.5.1 'I am the problem'.

Source: Reproduced with kind permission of the patient.

been masturbating. These are the memories that surfaced, but they were probably the tip of the iceberg of humiliation endured in various ways for the whole of childhood.

I have often had sex addicts who tell me that they had wonderful child-hoods, but these things can be deceptive. Experiences of humiliation impact on the development of the self in ways that are not forgotten. In such cases, there are sometimes family rules operating like 'do not talk badly of the family' or self-punishment beliefs operating, such as 'I deserved it. It did me no harm. I was a tearaway.' I never find it otherwise than that sexual addicts grow up with a deeply flawed sense of self. Sometimes it is so covered by their defences that they are incapable of seeing it or accepting it. I had a patient tell me, 'I have factories all over the world'. This, along with his metal American Express card, was his defence against shame. When he was sitting in the chair opposite me, I saw a boy of 12, an angry, hurt child, whose defence against shame had been to create a fortress of success.

It is not unusual for people to try to guard against feelings of shame through high achievement. Dr Stephen Pattison, a clergyman who specialised in Practical Theology at Cardiff University and is now at Birmingham University, wrote an excellent book on the nature of shame, named *Shame, Theory, Theology* (2000). He makes us aware that a constant drive for high achievement is sometimes accompanied by alcohol use, overeating, recreational drug use and sexual addiction. Sexual addiction provides a release mechanism from the demands of work and high achievement. Work is the control element of a cycle that alternates between control and release; sexual addiction can provide the release element of the cycle.

I have written about Wright in the book *CBT for Compulsive Behaviour – A Guide for Professionals* but I want to go more into his story here. Wright was disliked by his father. His mother was so damaged that she was never able to properly parent Wright. He grew up into a self-hating person. This level of self-hatred permeated everything. Although he was outwardly successful as a barrister, his life was tormented by self-doubt and self-reproach. He acted out on the internet and was powerfully attached to one female porn star. His sense of shame was so great that he believed that it was contributing to his downfall. In spite of all his outward success, he felt himself to be irredeemable. Slowly and painfully we tried to build up his sense of self-worth but the weight of the shame was greater than our resources could bear. But he went on, with courage and fortitude. I have never known a man to struggle with such heroism against the forces of darkness.

Sexual addiction may be an outworking of a deeply felt inner sense of shame but it is also the generator of ongoing shame. This is the catch. Sexual addiction is used as a shame reliever but it is also a mechanism for shame generation. In other words, I am ashamed and therefore I act out. Afterwards, acting out makes me feel shameful. I feel shame and I do shameful things and so the shame is compounded and becomes the proof that I am shameful. It is a vicious cycle: the escape route of sexual addiction confirms and escalates the deep-seated belief that I am shameful.

Many sex addicts find themselves stuck in a 'shame spiral' (Kaufman 1989). The shame spiral consists of an event which triggers endemic shame, followed by repetitive rumination on the shame event. These feelings and thoughts create a downward spiral of distress. The events are considered, over and over, and this increases the feelings of shame. Finally, the self is overcome with shame and a kind of paralysis occurs. For example, imagine you are caught by your partner who has looked at your phone and has found email correspondence with a sex worker. You feel an immense amount of shame. You relive this scene over and over in your mind so that the shame mounts up and up. The problem with this sequence of events is that shame is a major contributor to sexual acting out. The more shame you feel, the more intolerable it becomes. This takes you back to sexually acting out as the antidote to the feelings of shame. Alas, the shaming partner can unwittingly contribute to creating the next bout of sexually addictive behaviour.

Defences against shame

Gershen Kaufman, who was Professor in Counselling at the Department of Psychology at Michigan State University, suggests that people tend to adopt one or more of the following mechanisms to defend themselves from shame: rage, contempt, perfectionism, control, blaming others, internal withdrawal, humour and denial. He writes that 'rage protects the self against shame' (Kaufman 1989: 100). Contempt makes one better than and, therefore, above the other. Perfectionism is a response to feeling defective. We take control to keep ourselves safe. We blame others and make them shameful and this transfers the shame from us to them. Withdrawal is hiding from shame where only the superficial self is made known. It might be helpful to think about how you are constructed as a person and whether you use any of the defences listed above to manage shame.

Pattison (2000) tells us that there are four ways that we use to manage shame: withdrawal, avoidance, attack self and attack other. The withdrawal response involves just that, withdrawal. As I said earlier, the word 'shame' means 'hide'. This does not mean going into a cupboard and closing the door, but it can mean, for example, avoiding lunch, staying in your office and not mixing with others. I have a patient (not a sex addict) who does just that. He told me, 'I never feel that I belong'. The shame of going to a comprehensive school, surrounded now by the upper middle class with a private education, creates residual shame that is more powerful for him than his double first from Oxford. He hides. Avoidance is the typical way that the sex addict manages shame. You avoid the feelings with sexual activity. Alcohol does the same for some people. Others do it by overeating and this leads to weight gain. Being overweight in our society is shameful and so the avoidance mechanism actually contributes to the problem. I see the 'attack self' mechanism repeatedly in working with sex addicts. It is that often violent voice deep inside that says, 'I am no good and no one could possibly love me if they knew what I do'. Finally, there is the 'attack other' mechanism. I sometimes see this in sex addicts who are judgemental of others. The 'attack other' script motivates 'twitter trolls' and people who abuse others on the internet, and it motivates the journalism that took the tabloid newspaper to the gate of the house of my patient. We seek to reveal in others what we seek to conceal in ourselves.

Sometimes shame manifests in body dysmorphic disorder. This disorder, if we can call it that, is the overwhelming sense that there is something wrong with some part of our body. It sometimes presents with sexual addiction. It might present as 'I hate my ears' or 'I hate my nose'. Generally, though, with male sex addicts, it is a sense that there is something wrong with their penis. Many maintain that their penis is too small; this seems to me to be an outworking of the belief that 'I am diminished', which is somatised into 'my penis is too small'. Given the fact that the average porn star's penis is 3 inches longer than that of the average man, this fear would be reinforced by watching a lot of internet pornography. Shame can also emerge from real, rather than imagined, disorders. I have noted, not infrequently, that some men who are infertile tend to make up for this deficiency by being sexual with as many people as possible. Maybe this is just sexual addiction but it seems to me to be a way of expressing virility as a compensation for the absence of fertility. Just as people with body dysmorphic disorder tend to specialise in art and design as professional or vocational subjects (Veale *et al.* 2002), so it stands to reason that men preoccupied with sex would tend to focus on the penis as being deficient as a response to sexual shame. They give themselves the message, 'I am diminished and even my penis is too small'.

Healing shame

This discussion about shame brings me to the subject of treatment. The healing of shame is central to the treatment of the sexually addicted. The first stage in this process is to help you to develop an awareness of shame.

This is what this section is about. I have tried to write about shame so that you will understand it and begin to identify it. Awareness that you are experiencing feelings of shame is fundamentally different to being at the mercy of shame. This is especially true because the shame feelings are a legacy of the past and need not continue to operate in the future. These are automatic thoughts and feelings and it is possible to notice them but dismiss them as irrelevant to the present. Things that we understand do not govern us in the same way as things that we do not understand.

In the telling of shame to a non-shaming, non-judgemental other person, it is reduced. I have one patient who continually says, 'Exposure reduces shame'. We had a man in one of our recovery groups who was riddled with shame. It took him every effort just to turn up to a group. He spent a huge amount of time using internet pornography. He had two days off of work per week and he would start to use the internet on the morning of his first day off and finally come off of it in the evening of his second day off. During this whole period, he would be looking at internet pornography. At the second meeting of the group, he said that there was something that he had to tell them. He said that he had a mortifying habit of storing cans of his urine in his cupboard. While he was telling the group this, I could observe all his outward signs of shame: head down, eyes on the floor, body crouched over in the chair. I asked him if he wanted feedback from the group. Slowly, one by one, people in the group told him not to worry, they had things that they did, or had done, for which they too experienced mortal shame. The effect of this feedback was startling to see in the face and body of the man concerned. The shame had been wiped away. His bravery in the face of shame did a couple of things for the group. It gave others permission to talk about events that were shaming. It also gave them an opportunity to exercise kindness and altruism. In the exercise of kindness and altruism, both parties benefit. From that moment on, the group took on a new quality of life and became a cohesive force of change for all involved.

So, if shame dies on exposure, you might want to consider how you too can expose your own shame. Consider someone you know, with whom you would be able to share some of the things that have been hidden because of shame. Perhaps you might choose a close friend or a family member. Alternatively, you might choose someone who is not involved in your daily life. I would suggest that you go to this person, whoever it might be, and tell them that there is something that you need to tell them. Tell them that you do not need advice but you just need them to listen.

I had one patient who was plagued by shame and he finally called two reliable family members together to tell them about his sexual acting out.

I was present. His sister cried and his uncle offered to pay for his treatment. They loved him. His uncle reached out his hand out to him. The patient told me afterwards that this had never happened before. He texted me after the session to say that he felt at peace. Shame is reduced, even wiped out, on exposure to the light. There is no longer any need to live a double life or to hide the broken part of the self from others. In fact, we are all broken.

Earlier, I wrote about the shame set-up in my own life. To realise that it was a set-up was a major part of my own recovery. Yes, we all can feel shame but that is different to being shame-based. To be shame-based is to be constantly plagued by shame. It can give rise to perfectionism, the belief that 'I must be perfect'. To break free of this overwhelming and all-pervasive shame has been the single most important gift of the recovery process for me. Here is the promise that accompanies recovery: you will find new freedom and new happiness. This will always materialise if you work for it.

I shall make one concluding remark on the topic of shame: I recently went to see the film *Shame* co-written and directed by Steve McQueen. The film was well acted by Michael Fassbender playing Brandon and Carey Mulligan playing his sister, Sissy. I have never seen a film with so much explicit sex and nudity that was so completely without erotic appeal. Why? Because the film was about the shame of sexual addiction and the futility of a life so caught up in addictive compulsive behaviour.

Summarise what you have learned about shame:

_____

_____

_____

_____

_____

_____

_____

_____

_____

_____

Chapter 6

Neuroscience

Introduction

The neurochemistry that lies behind sexual addiction is complicated and it can be difficult to understand for the layman. However, there is a good reason for going into this subject in some detail. An understanding of the neurochemistry of addiction will reduce shame, because you will see that the repetition of sexual behaviour makes long-term changes in your brain that make it difficult for you to leave the behaviour behind.

We might like to consider addiction as an argument between your cognitive mind and your 'limbic system'. The limbic system is the threat centre of the brain. The cognitive mind says 'No, I am not going to do this', but the other part of the mind, under the influence of the arousal chemistry, says 'I really want this'. Frequent past repetition of the behaviour means that the part of the brain that is in favour of acting out often wins. The goal of recovery is for the part of the mind that says 'no' to triumph over the part of the mind that says 'yes'. This requires effortful practice and frequent intervention.

This chapter outlines the fundamental principles of the brain chemistry that lies behind sexual addiction. It considers how addiction disrupts clear thinking, negatively impacting upon our ability to consistently make choices which give us a better quality of life. We go for the short-term hit rather than for the longer-term creation of a better quality of life. This chapter explores four brain chemicals, namely DeltaFosB, vasopressin, serotonin and dopamine. We will also consider how positive changes in the brain can help us to overcome sexual addiction.

Let us start with the question of genetic predisposition towards addiction. While it is asserted that the tendency towards addiction has a genetic base, it is too easy, and not helpful, to blame your addiction on your genes. There is only a *tendency* towards an addictive pattern that might explain why some people are more likely to be addicted than others. Volkow and Li write that '40–60% of the vulnerability to addiction can be attributed to genetic factors' (Volkow and Li 2005: 1429). Similar figures are cited by other authorities. However, remember that it is just the tendency towards addiction that is genetic and not the actual presence of a substance addiction or of a repetitious behaviour. In working with sexually addicted men, one thing seems clear: there is often a family pattern of addictive behaviour. For our purposes, it does not seem important whether this is explained by genetics or by the inheritance of learned behaviours. However, it is important to recognise that we all inherit something and most of us have an obstacle in life that we need to work to overcome. A predisposition towards addiction, be it genetic or a legacy from the historic family dynamic, is important to understand. It reduces shame to know that you are vulnerable to sexual addiction not because you are morally deficient but because you are predisposed towards addiction either through genetic inheritance or though inter-familial patterns. The more that shame is reduced, the more that the drive to act out sexually is lessened.

I have observed that addictions can change from generation to generation. For example, if there is an alcoholic mother or father, this might transfer in the next generation as addiction to religion, where religious behaviour provides an alternative to alcoholism. Religion becomes a behavioural substitute for the use of substances. Alternatively, the children of religious parents can rebel and use substances and behaviours in an addictive fashion instead of religion. These comments are about the individual's relationship to a belief system and not about the content of any religious system.

Addiction as a biological drive

We need to keep in mind that sexual behaviour is much more than thinking and is not the product of logic. It is the product of a powerful in-built mechanism, the primary purpose of which is to maintain the species. You have one dominant biological mission and that is to maximise your DNA. Sexual behaviour is endowed by Mother Nature with force and power. There is very little in the realm of the human being that is more powerfully reinforced. I had a patient who went dogging (visiting car parks at night); he realised, driving home the next morning as the sun was coming up, that his dinner from the Chinese takeaway shop was still sitting on the floor of the car where he had put it the previous evening. Sex had triumphed over hunger.

Sexual need and romantic preoccupations can drive men and women to extreme and sometimes dangerous behaviour. When we are in love, the brain is filled with opioids which give us those glorious feelings. The cognitive part of the brain is distorted and often we do not think straight; we are endlessly preoccupied by thoughts of the beloved and have blissful feelings of merger. On the downside, our judgement is impaired and we cannot see any negative features in the beloved. We only become aware of these as time takes its course and the romantic chemistry dies down.

People find that it is not easy to resist and overcome the powerful biological drive behind sex. It can cause the most powerful to succumb to dangerous and personally harmful behaviour. I think of Bill Clinton. Whatever possessed him to have oral sex with Monica Lewinsky? Here is a man at the top of his professional life with every gift and everything to lose and he succumbed. Another case is that of Dominique Strauss-Kahn, a man of international importance. He too was overwhelmed by his sexual drive and the result was catastrophic for his reputation and his professional life. Another would be Stephen Green who, when he was the UK Director of Public Prosecution, was arrested for curb crawling near King's Cross Station in London. He lost everything. His wife committed suicide a year later. These men, who were successful and had reached the top of their professional life, were still subject to the relentless demands of sexual need.

Some experts argue that addiction is associated with impaired executive function. This means that addiction weakens our ability to use the thinking part of the brain. It disturbs the ability to initiate, plan and make rational value judgements. Arousal chemistry overwhelms cognitive function. The sexually addicted person goes for short-term gain and long-term loss. The person makes choices that invariably and repeatedly bring unhappiness and regret rather than choices that bring wellbeing and satisfaction. Men who have no problems with cognitive function in their working life seem not to make the same application to their sexual lives. This is the effect of addiction. It interferes with our ability to think, prioritise and plan. This is not just about weakness of will but about a neurochemical process in the brain that makes these actions difficult to achieve. The idea that behaviours have consequences is overshadowed in the immediacy of the anticipated hit. The short-term thrill is so exciting that it eclipses an awareness of the aftermath.

Imagine that you are sitting at your computer. You have an important report that is due tomorrow. You feel anxious about the report, you are bored while you are doing it and your partner is out of the house for the afternoon. Three things come together: need, boredom and opportunity. You think 'I will just go on to the internet for ten minutes'. Three hours later, having had an orgasm, you come off the internet. You feel awful because you have wasted three hours, you have not prepared the report and you have behaved in a way that you know would hurt your partner. The choice was made because the power and proximity of excitement looms much more powerfully than does the after-effect of shame and regret, even though the shame and regret might last for days and the erotic pleasure might last for minutes. Your mind seems not to function properly and you make the choice, a choice that brings with it much unhappiness, rather than the choice that will make you feel good: job accomplished, report prepared and conscience clear. Such is addiction. It is always about short-term gain and long-term loss.

I am going to go into detail about the neurochemistry of addiction because I want you to understand that addiction is a brain issue and not a matter of moral judgement or weak will. The brain has become patterned with the addictive responses. The repetition of sexual patterns and, in particular, the use of sexual behaviour to mitigate the effects of loneliness, anxiety and other kinds of distress causes 'plasticity' in the neural circuits in our brains which are related to reward and motivation. In other words, it actually changes the neural pathways in our brains and affects how information is transported through our nervous systems. Studies have shown that the brain is physically changed by repetitious learning, and addiction represents a powerful form of this (Hilton 2013). The use of addictive substances and behaviours create links between neurons in our brains, forming neural pathways that are reinforced by repetition. As we continue to repeat the behaviours, they become more driven and automatic (Ryan 2013). New brain structures develop that allow the behaviour to dominate in our lives. This supports the idea that addiction is a biological disorder located primarily in the brain.

Chemical dependency and sexual compulsivity share many of the same features. It is argued that sex activates the same neural pathways, in much the same way as alcohol and drugs (Ray 2012). The part of the brain that responds to substance use is the same part of the brain that responds to internet pornography (Reynaud *et al.* 2010). In other words, the brain mechanisms and neural circuits connected to substance use are the same ones that operate with sexual desire and orgasm. Neuroimaging data supports this assertion. Natural drives and substance-connected longing can hijack the brain's reward systems. Whilst alcohol and drugs are external agents in this process, sex is an internally generated chemical response.

The reward system in the brain that provides sexual pleasure is a very powerful one, perhaps even the most powerful. Through habitually turning to sex to self-soothe, brain organisation becomes sensitised to sexual stimuli and this heightens the response to sexual cues. These sexual cues acquire additional relevance to the sexually addicted individual. The patient who uses internet pornography for two to three hours every evening would find that this usage would sculpt his neural pathways in the same way as alcohol or other recreational drugs. To search on the internet and look for the perfect masturbatory image is an exercise in 'neuroplastic learning' (Hilton 2013). In other words, it actively shapes the neural pathways in your brain. Internet pornography addiction also has a powerful hold because it is rewarded on what is known as a 'variable ratio schedule'. You never quite know when you are going to come across that perfect image or clip. Some images will hit the spot while others will not be quite right. The rewards are just like the rewards of a slot machine. You can never predict when you will win or lose. Hits that come in a random sequence like these tend to be more addictive than those that come with predicted regularity (Maltz and Maltz 2008).

The American Society of Addictive Medicine defines addiction as a 'chronic disease of brain reward, motivation, memory and related circuitry' (ASAM no date). Addiction alters biology and, at its most fundamental, is as much about neuronal activity as it is about bad choices.

Brain chemistry

In order to understand why our brains respond to sexual stimulation in the way that they do, it is important to have a rudimentary knowledge of brain chemistry. There are four brain chemicals for us to understand that are important in addictive processes: DeltaFosB, vasopressin, dopamine and serotonin. In summary, DeltaFosB keeps you doing something even when you have stopped enjoying it, vasopressin is related to persistence and focus, dopamine creates pleasure, while serotonin is the 'feel good' chemical.

The role of DeltaFosB has not been extensively researched but there is growing evidence that it seems to be involved in the mediation of drug-related rewards. Research in animals has shown that high levels of Delta-FosB cause them to go for drugs like morphine and cocaine. Some other recent research has suggested a correlation between DeltaFosB and sexual behaviour. Sex is a highly rewarding behaviour and it is possible that various brain chemicals, and DeltaFosB in particular, may account for the persistence of the addictive process.

We can come to hate our addictive processes but go on doing them. I had a patient who used to masturbate many times a day and who told me that he didn't even enjoy it. I suspect that DeltaFosB was implicated in the continuation of a process that had ceased to actually give him pleasure. I am suggesting that changes in the brain caused by the repetition of sexually addictive patterns, such as the use of internet pornography, can create a rigid and enduring tendency to act out long after the pleasure of the behaviour has been left behind.

Let us turn to vasopressin. Oversimplifying a little, vasopressin is the brain chemistry of persistence and focus, and tends to predominate in men, peaking during sexual excitement. The eminent neuroscientist, Jan Panksepp, asserts that vasopressin is involved in male persistence (which is good for hunting), courtship, territory-marking and male aggression (which is good for fighting) (Panksepp 1998). It is also present in women in lower quantities, allowing them to protect their children from dangerous and aggressive outsiders (hence the term 'tiger-mothers').

As a man, I am personally aware of the persistent and focused nature of the male sexual drive. As I wrote earlier, it can broadly be asserted that women attract and men are attracted. The more persistent and focused you are, the more likely you are to maximise the dissemination of your DNA.

Most of the men seeking treatment at our clinic are focused and high achieving. This may only say something about the men who come for treatment at our specific clinic. However, it also suggests to me that these men may have higher overall levels of vasopressin than their peers. I am not sure that there is a correlation between sexual addiction and high achievement but if there is, it might be down to the naturally occurring levels of vasopressin in these men.

It is worth noting that there appears to be a clear relationship between our childhood experiences and our brain's susceptibility to developing addictive patterns. Hudson-Allez (2009) explains that childhood trauma corrupts the working of an internal mechanism called the 'hypothalamic-pituitary-adrenal axis' and this predisposes us to future addictive disorders. By trauma, she does not mean being beaten with a stick, but rather situations that were shaming, non-nurturing or neglectful. These are rarely one-off events but can be made up of a childhood of endless criticism and reproof without physical affection or without supportive nurturing. Hudson-Allez also states that early stress can create changes in the levels of vasopressin and oxytocin (the bonding hormone). This disposes us to have increased sexual arousal, decreased sexual fulfilment and problems committing to one lifelong partner. In the treatment programmes that I run, I find that most sex addicts experience all three of these features.

The third brain chemical for us to consider is dopamine. It is widely accepted that dopamine is an important chemical in regulating our experience of pleasure, and the use of drugs of abuse increases dopamine.

Research has shown that compulsive behaviours have the same effect. When dopamine levels increase in the brain, higher levels of reward are experienced.

Maltz and Maltz, authors of *The Porn Trap* (2008), state that dopamine is released during sexual arousal and that it produces an effect similar to crack cocaine. They write that, 'even the brief delay between clicking the mouse and the picture coming up on the computer screen can release dopamine' (Maltz and Maltz 2008: 19). Kingston and Firestone write that 'similarities between neurological substrates of addiction (e.g. dopamine dysregulation) and sexual appetitive behaviours have been identified to support the inclusion of sexual activity as a behavioural manifestation of addiction' (Kingston and Firestone 2008: 291).

Part of the evidence of the role of dopamine in sexual appetitive behaviour comes from dopamine-enhancing drugs used in the treatment of Parkinson's disease. Patients treated with these drugs can show increases in hypersexual behaviour. Dopamine seems to provide a foundation for sexual motivation and sexual activity.

The final brain chemical of concern to us here is serotonin, which is responsible for general wellbeing. It accounts for those pleasurable feelings that come over us after we have completed a major achievement. We might experience it after we go to the gym or return from a run. Serotonin actually reduces the need to act out sexually because when you feel good, there is no need to escape into another world.

This information comes from animal and human studies and from observing the role of selective serotonin reuptake inhibitors (SSRIs), which are the medications that are often used to treat depression. Kafka (1997), a medical doctor and researcher at Harvard, states that studies have demonstrated a connection between serotonin reduction and an increase in sexual behaviour. If this is the case, we might want to consider how to create higher levels of serotonin when trying to tackle sexual addiction. It is possible to create higher levels of serotonin naturally by participation in meaningful and enjoyable activities. This includes things like singing, dancing and physical exercise. Running is a natural response to danger and gives a real lift to the day ahead. I always run in the morning, as well as before any major event that requires me to be on top form, like giving a talk or presentation. When I took my viva for my doctoral studies, I went for a long run before the examination. The best exercise that has ever filled me with endorphins is boxing. Because I trained with a trainer, not only did I get a hit from training but I always won, giving me a double hit. Being in a cohesive group also releases serotonin, which is why I recommend groups to help people deal with addiction.

Many people find that SSRIs, which act by increasing the levels of serotonin in the brain, decrease libido. This can bring real relief to those who are acting out in a relentless secession of sexual behaviours. Treating some men with an SSRI seems to reduce sexual compulsivity and the intensity of the drive. It is important to note that some researchers have also found that this medication has no significant effects on partnered sex (Muench *et al.* 2011; Wainberg *et al.* 2006). In our clinic, we recommend SSRIs when compulsive sexual behaviour is accompanied by insistent repetitious thought processes or if the behaviour is dangerous and likely to be harmful to others, as well as endangering the sex addict himself.

Changing our brains

It used to be thought that the brain was fixed in its development. In other words, that once it had developed, that was all there was to it, nothing much would happen apart from later-life decline. However, recent research has demonstrated that the brain is quite plastic and that it can be changed by new learning. The learning involves repetition, frequency and duration. The more frequently you practise a new behaviour, the more persistently it is practised and the longer it is practised, the more likely it is that new neuropathways will emerge. We have already seen how this happens in a negative way to form addictions, but it can also be a positive process, which releases us from those same addictions. With practice, it is possible to create different responses to long-standing stimuli. Instead of using sex to self-soothe, it is possible to develop new, healthy responses to the triggers for sexual addiction that become almost automatic. This is difficult to start with but the more it is practised, the easier it becomes. I see this in the sexual addiction recovery groups we run at our clinic. At the start of the treatment programme there are frequent lapses, but over time these new alternative behaviours become easier to put in place and easier to promote. Sexual addiction can be replaced by new responses that, in the long term, give greater fulfilment and are less troubling to your quality of life.

Let me give a personal example of neuroplasticity. I was on the South Bank in London one day when I saw a group of people swing dancing. I liked the look of it and took one of the leaflets they were handing out. I decided that I needed dance in my life. I went to the first lesson and I was terrible. There was no place in my brain that linked music and movement. I was clumsy and everything felt strange. I had to fight an overwhelming sense of shame. I repeated the steps for two years (an example of the importance of frequency, repetition and duration). Eventually it came naturally to me and I could begin to do the steps without thinking about them. My teacher noticed that I was learning steps more quickly. What had happened? I had generated a whole new set of neuropathways by practice and repetition. There is an expression in neuroscience that 'neurons that fire together wire together'. This is what had happened. The same process is true when trying to leave behind unwanted sexual behaviours. It is like learning to dance when you haven't danced before. You have to practise new self-soothing mechanisms in a dedicated manner. After a while these new methods become second nature and they are automatically adopted, taking the place of sexual acting out.

So, in conclusion, sex addiction is not about the genitals, it is about a learned pattern of behaviour that shapes the way the brain is structured. Through frequency and repetition, our brains develop a biological predisposition to the behaviour. However, we can also make use of frequency and repetition to replace these behaviours with healthier alternatives.

Summarise what you have learned about neuroscience:

_____

_____

_____

_____

_____

_____

_____

_____

_____

_____

Chapter 7

Attachment

In trying to understand the reasons behind our sexual addiction, it is important to have an understanding of the concept of 'attachment'. Attachment refers to the way we connect to other people and, in particular, to the way we connect in our intimate relationships. Our attachment style is set up in childhood and reflects the way in which we attached to our parents or caregivers. There are four possible attachment styles: secure, avoidant, anxious and disorganised. The securely attached person received good enough parenting with appropriately responsible parents. There was a healthy interaction between caregiver and the child. The secure child can form secure relationships as an adult and is good at managing his own emotional states. The avoidant attachment style is a response to indifferent, absent or abusive patterns of the caregiver to the child. The child simply avoids the caregiver. He has learned that to be safe, he has to rely upon himself. He is likely to grow into an adult who avoids too much emotional commitment and who goes to great lengths to avoid experiencing difficult emotional states. Alternatively, with the same situation, the child can become needy and anxious about the loss of the caregiver. In his adult relationships, he is likely to be needy and clingy, worrying that his partners will leave him. The child with a disorganised attachment style lives in perpetual fear or anger and this results in the formation of seriously disturbed individuals in later life.

I have summarised below another way of explaining attachment styles that is easy to understand and remember. It was formulated by Bartholomew and Horawitz (1991).

SECURE: I am okay and you are okay.
AVOIDANT: I am okay and you are not okay.
ANXIOUS: You are okay and I am not okay.
DISORGANISED: You are not okay and I am not okay.

Our basic attachment styles stay with us for life unless we recognise them and deliberately try to intervene in them, or unless we come into a relationship with another who has the capacity to make up for the earlier deficiencies in the relationship with the caregivers.

I have done some research on my own attachment style. I am half avoidant and half secure. I am avoidant because I do my own thing without much consultation and I take care of myself. I do not want or expect others to do this for me. I am secure in so far as I have been capable of a long-term relationship with another person. Only a bit of me is disorganised.

The reason I am going into this in detail is because attachment styles are related to addiction and therefore to sexual addiction. Most sex addicts have an avoidant attachment style and they disappear into sexual activity to avoid miserable feelings states, to get 'me' time or to soothe an otherwise intolerable feeling state. Sometimes men have an anxious attachment style and stay in abusive relationships because the alternative abandonment seems too horrible to manage. But, for the most part, sexually addicted men tend to have an avoidant attachment style.

Glynn Hudson-Allez (2009), the author of *Infant Losses, Adult Searches* and an experienced clinical psychologist, writes that avoidant persons have reduced oxytocin. Oxytocin is the brain chemical of human bonding. This would, in part, explain why such people are less likely to have strong, lasting relationships. People with avoidant attachment styles might use substances and behaviours as external sources of self-regulation. Another researcher, Katehakis (2016), recognises that sex addicts easily operate in a one-person system and that they continue in one-person behaviours, such as sexual addiction, to self-soothe. The person with an anxious attachment style has difficulty moderating extreme feelings and therefore looks to behaviours and substances to do this for them.

Once you understand that this dysfunctional regulation was set up in childhood, there is a reduction in shame because you are not responsible for having the problem. However, you are responsible for what you do about it.

Summarise what you have learned about attachment:

_____

_____

_____

_____

_____

_____

_____

_____

_____

_____

Review of the tasks for the preliminary week

- Read about cognitive behavioural therapy, sexual addiction, supernormal phenomena, shame, neuroscience and attachment.
- Prepare and keep the urge diary.
- Recite the introductory pillar three times a day.

You might also:

- Order one of the recommended books.
- Browse through listings for other useful books.
- Look up Sex Addicts Anonymous or Sex and Love Addicts Anonymous.
- Read their literature.
- Print out a meeting list.

Part II

10-week recovery programme

Core belief and formulation

Introduction

Not long ago, my patient Jimmy told me that he had 'found himself acting out in Soho', in London. I challenged this statement as, surely, there must have been a series of events and decisions that took him there. Jimmy lived in Streatham, about 10 miles away from Soho. He would have had to take a bus, choose a destination, change to the underground, decide upon a direction to walk in and, once there, he would have had the option to turn around. The process of getting from Streatham to Soho involves a series of thoughts, feelings and behaviours. Of course, Jimmy was on automatic pilot and was unaware of this. He had repeated the process so many times that the steps involved were built into his system. His acting out patterns had become automatic and out of awareness.

We can draw parallels between Jimmy's unconscious processes and driving a car. Once you learn how to drive, it becomes unconscious. You do not have to think about changing gears, pressing the accelerator or braking at a roundabout. The thoughts behind these actions become automatic. This is an excellent thing for driving, but it is less helpful when considering out of control sexual behaviour. It is therefore important for you to begin to gain a greater understanding of the sequence of thoughts and feelings that lead to your acting out behaviour.

People often act out sexually as a way to escape distress. It is a self-soothing mechanism. So, in this first week of the recovery programme, we will begin by analysing the situations and events that you find distressing, disturbing or upsetting. By looking at the events that upset you, and analysing your thoughts, feelings and behaviours, we will be able to uncover your 'core beliefs'. The core belief is a deeply held view of yourself which might well have been lost to your vision of yourself. Most of us defend ourselves against the implications of our core beliefs with a whole retinue of management techniques.

The second thing that we are going to do this week is to try to help you to make your own formulation. The formulation is just a way of trying to bring some order and sense to what probably seems like a confused situation that is difficult to understand. The formulation is simply a diagram which describes your situation and, in particular, the fundamentals of the problem of sexually compulsive behaviour.

Uncovering your core belief

In order to work out what your core beliefs are, we are going to examine events and thoughts that have upset you and then make a diagram of the problem. You can use the template provided to help you (see Table 2.1.1). I would like you to begin by thinking of three real situations that upset you recently. They might have occurred at work, on the bus or driving the car, or perhaps they are things that happened at home or with your partner. Note each of these situations in the table, describing the crucial elements of the event and labelling it for ease of identification.

One of my key tasks as your CBT therapist is to alert you to the automatic thoughts which lie behind your attitudes, feelings and responses. These are the thoughts that flash through your mind so quickly in response to a situation that you hardly even register them. They affect the interpretation and meaning that you place upon a situation. The specific interpretation that each of us makes about an event may differ from that which other people would make. Our own way of thinking is shaped by our upbringing, our culture and our experiences. Yet when we find automatic thoughts flashing through our heads, we are generally unaware of all of these factors, just accepting the thought as the true interpretation of the event. As we saw in Chapter 2, these thoughts go on to shape the way we feel about the event, as well as the way that we behave.

Table 2.1.1 Identifying core beliefs

	Upsetting event 1	Upsetting event 2	Upsetting event 3
Situation			
Automatic thoughts			
Emotion			
Behaviour			
Meaning/core belief			

So, I would now like you to consider the 'automatic' thoughts that you have in each of the three upsetting situations that you noted down in the table. Make a note of the thoughts that went through your mind during each event. Keep in mind we are talking now about thoughts and not feelings. The feelings follow the thoughts.

Once you have noted the thoughts, think about the emotions that you had at the time and note them down. There are really only four relevant emotions: anxiety, shame, anger and loss. Anything else you might write is a euphemism for one of these four feelings. For example, frustration is probably mild anger. In our society, men are often socialised out of feelings, with some feelings thought to be unmanly. For example, feelings of fear are universal, yet men have been taught that they must not show fear. Anger, however, is socially supported as an appropriate feeling state for men. Women, on the other hand, are socialised to show fear and not to show anger. But we all have these different feeling states and it is really important that we learn to recognise them if we are to be able to break the addiction cycle. In our treatment programme we encourage men to be open with their feelings. You need to learn to know what is happening inside of you. So now, write down the emotions you experienced in each of the three upsetting situations, giving them a score from 1 to 10, in terms of their intensity.

Then, go on to consider the behaviours. The behaviours can be really big, like screaming at the top of your voice, or really small, like the loss of eye contact with the other person. They can be single or multiple, for example loss of eye contact and frowning, head shaking or changing the facial expression to indifference or hostility. Keep in mind that we need to notice all behaviours, some of which we are almost unaware of. There might have been changes in tone or volume of the voice, small changes in speech or body language, as well as larger behaviours like running out of the room or putting your fist through the door. The upset is often accompanied by physical changes in the body; these might include an upset stomach, racing heart, tightness in the chest, breathlessness or sweaty palms, so make a note if you experienced any of these.

When you have done this, you can move onto the most important part. CBT not only looks at thoughts, but also focuses on the meaning of these thoughts, uncovering the core beliefs that underpin them. The core belief is a deeply held view of yourself, usually formed in early childhood. It tends to be rigid and inflexible. It can sometimes be difficult to access and identify because of family messages and because most of us have spent a lifetime trying to disguise it or avoid it. Most of us defend our self against the implications of the core belief with a whole retinue of management techniques.

Let me give you an example of my own core belief and how I can access it using the structure for analysing the thoughts, feelings and behaviours that we looked at above. The relevant situation was 'hearing that someone was more successful than me'. My thought was 'she is really going for it'. My feelings were resentment and shame. My behaviours were bad-mouthing her to my secretary. Now we need to look at the meaning behind the thoughts. In my case, it was 'I am not good enough'. This is my core belief, which had been triggered by hearing about her success. I could have had more benign thoughts like 'good on her, she is going for it' or 'there are ups and downs in anyone's professional life'. The thought that struck me, though, was 'she is more than me because I am not enough'. This thought trumped the others precisely because it resonated with my core belief.

In order to uncover your own core beliefs, take a look at the automatic thoughts that you have noted in the table and consider the following questions:

- What was the meaning of the thought to me?
- What does that thought say about my view of myself?

Once you think you have the answers, note them down in the table.

Let me give you some examples from patients I have seen, to help you with this table.

Richard did this exercise and noted the following content:

SITUATION: My partner called me lazy.
AUTOMATIC THOUGHTS: This is unfair. I cooked dinner yesterday.
EMOTION: Anger at 8.
BEHAVIOUR: I sulked and went silent.
MEANING/CORE BELIEF: I am being mistreated. I am the kind of person who is mistreated. What kind of person is that? A weak person.

Tom did this exercise and noted the following content:

SITUATION: My kids are talking back to me.
AUTOMATIC THOUGHTS: I am being disrespected.
FEELINGS: Anger at 6.
BEHAVIOUR: I shout, my face gets contorted and looks fierce, I shake my hands in aggression.
MEANING/CORE BELIEF: I am not worth much.

Margie did this exercise and she worked it out like this:

SITUATION: My husband is always complaining that the kitchen is a mess.
AUTOMATIC THOUGHTS: I must be a terrible housekeeper.
FEELINGS: Shame at 7.
BEHAVIOUR: I cried.
MEANING/CORE BELIEF: I am not worth much as a mother and wife.

This was Jamie's situation:

SITUATION: Another car cut in front of me.
AUTOMATIC THOUGHTS: He is an idiot. Who does he think he is?
FEELINGS: Anger at 10.
BEHAVIOUR: I shouted and swore at him and made a gesture with my
    right hand.
MEANING/CORE BELIEF: I am being disrespected and this means that I am
    the kind of person that others disrespect.

In each of the cases above, the person jumped to a conclusion based on
their sense of self. These conclusions included 'I am not being respected'
and 'I am not a good person'. Not one of these people jumped to other
more benign explanations, such as 'Kids will be kids; after all she is 13', 'I
am a perfectly good mother. He is just a bit OCD' or 'The other driver has
his own issues and there is no need for me to take it personally'. In each
case the person jumped to a conclusion that reflected an inner fear that
they were, somehow, not measuring up or not thought to be measuring up.

It can be difficult to access because most of us have spent a lifetime
trying to disguise it or avoid it. However, the more we become aware of
the meaning that lies behind our interpretation of events, the closer we will
get to our core belief. This is important because usually our core belief
generates the difficult feelings of shame and, as we saw earlier, shame is a
primary driver of compulsive sexual behaviour.

Making a formulation

Once you have become adept at identifying your automatic thoughts and
the core beliefs that underlie these, you are ready to start making a formulation. A formulation is simply a diagrammatic outline of your situation
which, in this case, sets out the fundamentals of the problem of your sexually compulsive behaviour. It is a useful tool to help you understand the
legacy of the past and how that shapes your current behaviour.

The formulation is set out as a simple model, which is divided into four sections. These are: set-up, core belief, management techniques and escape mechanisms.

The set-up for the behaviour is the historical situation which set the framework for it, and usually occurs in childhood. Next comes the core belief. Most sex addicts have the core belief that they are not OK, that they are intrinsically flawed or somehow are not measuring up to expectations. This is then managed by behaviours and attitudes that are designed to disguise the core belief. These management techniques are usually expressed as if/then statements, for example, 'If I am friendly, then people will like me'. Because the core belief is accompanied by intolerable feelings of shame, there must be ways to escape from these feelings. We refer to these as escape mechanisms. Some people use sexual behaviour and fantasy as their escape mechanism. Most sex addicts have a formulation that looks like this:

Set-up: in the family
Core belief: 'I am not good'
Management techniques: work/keeping fit
Escape mechanism: sexual behaviour

Here is an extreme example. Hank used sex workers almost every day after work. On his way home he would stop off at a massage parlour where he would have an erotic massage from two or three women simultaneously. This was an expensive process and he had stolen over £100,000 to pay for this use of sex workers. He was eventually found out and arrested for embezzlement. His use of sex workers had been going on at this rate for three years. The clue to the behaviour can be found in his history. Hank did not have a good start in life. He was born not breathing and had to be resuscitated. His mother was in hospital for many weeks after his birth and he was never breastfed. His mother remained remote and disconnected from him throughout his early life. He came from a rigid and formal family and he was sent away to boarding school when he was seven years old. The school he attended was rigid and formal. He did not flourish in the school environment and there were behavioural problems. All of this set up a limitless yearning for female contact. The use of multiple sex workers simultaneously, the frequency of the behaviour and his heedlessness to the risks involved all seem to represent the extent and the urgency of this patient's addictive process. All of this was driven by his core belief, which was 'I am not worth much'.

Hank's formulation would look like this: the set-up was clearly in the family of origin, and particularly in the disturbed relationship with his mother. There was never any bonding, caused by his mother's illness as well as the difficult circumstances around his birth. This was increased by having a critical and judgemental father and then going away to boarding school. This gave rise to his core belief: 'I am not loved or looked after and it must be my fault. I am defective'. He defended himself against this by academic work and had two degrees, one in medical science and one in business studies. He used sexual behaviour to escape from the shame that emerged from his core belief.

His formulation looks something like this:

Set-up: family and school
Core belief: I am worthless
Management technique: if I am successful at business then I am good enough
Escape mechanism: sexual behaviour

It is easy to see how this combination came to be and how the components are all interconnected. Most addicts have a combination that looks something like the one above. The set-up can differ in detail but it is almost always caused by deficits in parenting and emerges from the family of origin. The management strategies differ from person to person. Typical management strategies might be: 'If I make money, then I am acceptable', 'If I can pull women, then I am desirable', 'If I smile all the time, then people will like me and that means I am acceptable'. In this book, we are concerned specifically with the use of sexual behaviour as an escape mechanism, but it is important to note that there are other escape mechanisms, such as recreational drugs, food, work and religion.

I will give you my own formulation as another example. The set-up for my behaviour was in the family. I was not good enough for my father and my mother was so damaged that she was indifferent to me. This set up a core belief that I am defective. My management techniques are being nice to everyone and the collection of diplomas. If I am nice, then people will like me. If I have enough diplomas, then I am acceptable. My escape mechanisms were sex, religion, food and alcohol. Once I understood this, the addiction began to lose its power. Now I know that when I feel shame, it is just that my core feeling of shame has been triggered and not that I am, in fact, shameful. This understanding has created a wonderful recognition and has been the platform of great liberation.

Figure 2.1.1 gives a frequently occurring formulation for someone who is sexually compulsive. Read through it carefully and then consider making a unique formulation that outlines your own distinctive combination, using the

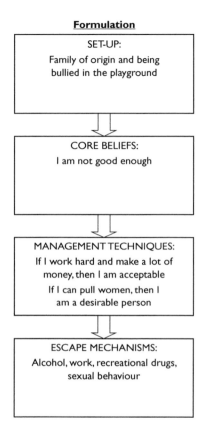

Formulation

SET-UP:

Family of origin and being
bullied in the playground

CORE BELIEFS:

I am not good enough

MANAGEMENT TECHNIQUES:

If I work hard and make a lot of
money, then I am acceptable

If I can pull women, then I
am a desirable person

ESCAPE MECHANISMS:

Alcohol, work, recreational drugs,
sexual behaviour

Figure 2.1.1 Sex addict's formulation.

form provided. Take some quiet time for yourself; go somewhere you can think about yourself without disturbance. I have provided a handy blank form for you to make your personal formulation (see Figure 2.1.2). You may find that you have to have another attempt at producing your individual formulation again later on in the recovery programme for it to make sense.

As you become clearer about your own formulation, you will be able to use it to notice the triggers that set you off down a path of sexually compulsive behaviour. This awareness will help you to begin to make different choices and to develop a healthier view of yourself, others and the world around you. This healthier view will no longer require you to use sexual behaviours to manage difficult emotions.

Formulation

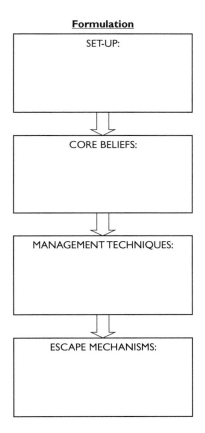

Figure 2.1.2 Personal formulation.

Recap of tasks for week 1 of the recovery programme

- Fill in the Upsetting Events table and work out your core belief.
- Make your formulation.
- Recite Pillar 1 three times a day.

Pillar for week 1

Now that I have started this process of change, it is important that I pursue it with application. I have applied myself to my sexually compulsive behaviours for a long time. Now I am learning how to apply myself to recovery. Application involves determination and endurance. It involves the determination to make the necessary changes to get the long-term results I desire, namely a life free of sexually compulsive behaviour. Application first means continuing with the programme outlined in this book. It means doing the exercises with diligence and continuing with them even though I do not really feel like doing them. Application means giving myself over to change. It also means making an application, as in applying for a job. It is in both senses that I make this application. I am applying for a new way of life and this involves application.

This week's learning summary:

_____

_____

_____

_____

_____

_____

_____

_____

_____

_____

Values clarification

Your value system

This week you are going to focus on the clarification of your value system. In other words, we will explore your values and the way in which they are enacted in your daily life. In her book, *Understanding and Treating Sexual Addiction*, UK sex addiction specialist Paula Hall writes that values are 'principles in our life from which we derive meaning and fulfilment' (Hall 2013: 94).

Our actions do not always follow our stated values. For example, I place a high value on generosity and openness, but I do not always give to the beggars who line the streets between my office and the tube station. I sometimes go past without even giving them a thought. I value courtesy but I do not always treat people courteously. I walked out of a restaurant the other day because I did not like the way the food was served. That would not have been a problem in itself, but I was not very courteous to the staff working there. I also value kindness, but I was not very kind to the Ugandan who came to see me about his sexual problems.

There is often a gap between our value system and our actions when it comes to our sexual behaviour. We might claim to value men and women, and yet exploit the needy and the weak. Take prostitution as an example. While some see sex work as a 'trade-off' or an exchange of goods and services, if the power imbalance is too great, the trade-off can turn into exploitation. This can work both ways, with women exploiting the sexual weakness in men for their own financial advancement. I think of the woman I wrote about earlier, who sold her story to the tabloid newspaper: in this case, who was the exploited and who was the exploiter? If you hold honesty as a major value but are lying to your wife about where you have been and the person you have been with, then you are not living according to your values. Pornography can also contradict our personal value systems. Some think that pornography inherently devalues its participants; it might also interfere or contradict our value system in other ways.

Perhaps the best real guide to our system of values can be taken from our behaviours. Our behaviours often betray our real values. Have a think about how your behaviours confirm or contradict your value system. There are two overriding problems with sexually compulsive behaviour: it often makes you feel shameful and it wastes a great deal of time. Participants in our treatment programme tell me that the biggest loss to them is the sheer amount of time wasted on sexual pursuits. The shame that you feel might be about the double life that you are leading, it might be about the loss of sexual interest in your partner or it might just be because there is so much conflict with your personal value system.

A useful way of thinking about your values is to write your own obituary. Sit down with a couple of sheets of paper and write out how you would like to be remembered. Of course, come the day, whoever will do the eulogy will only say nice things or at least put the difficult aspects of your character into more appealing language. If you are bitter and twisted as a person, they might describe you as challenging. I had a colleague once who was described in her reference as a 'gadfly'. I thought this meant that she was challenging. It turned out to mean that she was bad tempered and obstructive.

Let's look at some examples of how sexual addiction conflicted with some of my clients' values. William came to therapy because he spent substantial amounts of time using internet pornography. I gave him a list of values and asked him to select the five which were most important to him. He chose self-esteem, knowledge, nurturance, order and God. When he thought about his behaviour, he found that it contradicted his value system. Self-esteem was contradicted because his acting out behaviours actually lowered his sense of self-worth. Knowledge was also contradicted because he was wasting time on the internet while he was supposed to have been researching a paper he was writing. The behaviour also violated his value of nurturance in several ways. He was sexually absent from his partner and she found that this caused her to question her own desirability as a woman. He did not spend much time with his children because much of his time was spent on the internet. He was even not nurturing himself because the paper that was meant to advance his career was not being written. His internet behaviour also contributed to disorder in his life, rather than order. Late nights, bad sleep and rushed mornings all contributed to a sense that he was living in chaos, rather than in a healthy rhythm of work and leisure. And finally, there was God. William was a churchgoer and a believer of sorts, and yet he had a deep feeling that his behaviour was contrary to his public persona and his system of faith. On every count, the values that William felt to be right were contradicted by his use of internet pornography. For William, internet pornography had become an addiction. He was using it increasingly frequently to handle anxiety and all the time the use of internet pornography contributed to his discomfort. In the end, after doing this exercise, William realised that his life had become counterfeit. He resolved to make a change and to bring his actions into line with his beliefs and values.

When I asked another client, Robert, to select his top five values, he chose monogamy, wealth, tradition, authority and fitness. The value of monogamy was contradicted by cheating on his wife for over 20 years. His wealth was diminished by the fact that he had spent £1.5 million on sex workers over the 20-year period. His love of tradition was not much affected by his use of sex workers, but his authority was undermined by his double life. At one level, he knew that he was acting in a way that would not be respected. Robert had always been a sportsman and as a young man had been captain of the rugby team, but he was aware that he had gone to seed. He had put on a great deal of weight which, while not directly attributable to his use of sex workers, contributed to his low self-worth. If only he had gone for a run or to the gym, rather than acting out with sex workers, this might not have been the case.

The above two examples illustrate the violation of values by the use of internet pornography and the use of sex workers. In Robert's case, some of these violations were indirect. But no matter how you frame it, Robert was leading a life that impoverished his sense of self. William's problem was more direct and consequential and he too was living in contradiction to his professed values. To live in a way that opposes your value system creates problems and reduces self-dignity. The trouble might not happen immediately, or all at once, but it slowly undermines a sense of personal integrity.

The word 'value' comes from the same Latin root as valiant or valour. It means 'be strong, be well', or 'be of value'. The function of this recovery programme is to build strength and wellness. Let us go to the other side of the meaning of the word. It also requires strength and determination to make the necessary changes. I know that I am asking you to begin to make a significant behavioural change. It will not happen at once, but it will happen, if you work for it.

Exercise: values clarification

I would suggest that you now take time out to consider your own values. I have laid out a list of predominating values that some of us hold dear (see Table 2.2.1). I would like you to read through the list and mark your top five values.

Table 2.2.1 Values list

Dependability	Romance	Achievement	Faithfulness
Compassion	Autonomy	Hope	Loving
Self-control	Industry	Family	Mastery
Openness	Courtesy	Purpose	World peace
Self-awareness	Leisure	Sexuality	Generosity
Tolerance	Responsibility	Service	Duty
Independence	Comfort	Loved	Moderation
Honesty	Friendship	Humility	Helpfulness
Justice	Creativity	Simplicity	Solitude
Spirituality	Power	Safety	Self-acceptance
Beauty	Intimacy	Fun	Cooperation
Inner peace	Fitness	Change	Challenge
Growth	Flexibility	Excitement	Caring
Knowledge	Adventure	Self-esteem	Acceptance
Fame	Wealth	Virtue	Risk taking
Nurturance	Monogamy	Non-conformity	Order
Passion	Genuine	Popularity	Feeling good
Stability	Tradition	Commitment	Health
God	Forgiveness	Authority	Attractiveness

Source: Adapted from CASAA (2015).

Once you have chosen your five top values, I would like you to think about your sexual behaviour and, using the template provided, write out how your sexual behaviour confirms or contradicts your dearly held values. You might like to discuss values with people who are important to you and perhaps read up some more on values.

Value 1 _____
How does my sexual behaviour confirm or contradict this value?

_____

_____

_____

_____

_____

Value 2 _____
How does my sexual behaviour confirm or contradict this value?

_____

_____

_____

_____

_____

Value 3 _____
How does my sexual behaviour confirm or contradict this value?

_____

_____

_____

_____

_____

Value 4 _____
How does my sexual behaviour confirm or contradict this value?

_____

_____

_____

_____

_____

Value 5 _____
How does my sexual behaviour confirm or contradict this value?

_____

_____

_____

_____

_____

Recap of tasks for week 2

- Exercise: Values Clarification.
- Continue to keep the urge diary.
- Recite Pillar 2 three times a day.

You may also wish to reread some of the preliminary chapters in this book, in order to refresh your memory.

Pillar for week 2

Values are a distinctly human possession. I do not think that animals actually have values but rather instincts. It is not that they cannot feel emotion but to have aspirational standards for living is a culmination of the human character. There is great nobility in the pursuit of values. I see this for my own dignity and for the wellbeing of my children, my partner, my colleagues and the wider society. When I observe that my stated values are undermined by my actual behaviour, this calls into question the dignity of my personhood. I will now try to bring my value system and the reality of my behaviour into line with each other. I can do this, and in the doing of it, I am able to change and become a person whose actions match his words.

This week's learning summary:

_____

_____

_____

_____

_____

_____

_____

_____

_____

_____

Harmful consequences and worst case scenario

Sexually compulsive behaviour can be pleasurable both in the preparation of the act and in the doing of it. The pleasure is in the intensity of the build-up, the loss of self in the act, the power of the orgasm and the alleviation of any negative feeling states that preceded it. We are biologically programmed to be sexual and the brain chemistry of arousal shuts down cognitive function. Sexual addiction is a short-term, powerfully rewarded behaviour. The reward is so powerful that its strength often eclipses any negative after-effects of the behaviour.

However, the reality is that sexual acting out often does have harmful consequences and does nothing to generate long-term wellbeing. After the experience is over, there is nothing to show for it. Nothing has been achieved. You go back to the same feeling states that you were initially trying to alleviate, usually with the added woe of wasted time and increased shame. It does nothing to generate long-term wellbeing.

You probably recognise the situation that I am trying to explain. You come off the internet, out of the massage parlour or out of the sex worker's flat, not feeling very good. Perhaps you can hardly wait until she leaves the hotel room. I remember a patient defining 'eternity' as the time between the orgasm and the taxi.

Let me tell you about some of the harmful consequences that the clients in my clinical practice have experienced. There is Thomas, who is currently on remand in prison for exposing himself on a bus. There is also Robert, who had been cautioned by the police for exposing himself on a train. Adrian was arrested for looking at underage pornography. This happened under the influence of alcohol and cocaine. He was not a paedophile but these two substances took away his normal braking system and he ventured into the illegal. He was sent to prison for two weeks. He lost his business and 30 families lost their livelihood. Another patient, who was an expert with computers, had been file sharing. Little did he know that illegal material had been downloaded onto his computer. That did not stop the police from prosecuting him. These are all serious negative consequences of sexually compulsive behaviour.

There was Roy, who was in a relationship with two women. One was his wife, with whom he had two daughters. He loved the other woman too and had one son with her. When his wife found out about them, everyone was in turmoil. I spent many hours with him and his anguish was dreadful to watch. There was also Nigel, who only acted out on the internet in hotel rooms when he travelled on business. Once or twice he had gone beyond the internet to setting up a meeting with a sex worker. His wife found his phone and discovered the infidelities. She was devastated. He has been in treatment now for six months and the distress at home has hardly lessened.

You may not be arrested for your compulsive sexual behaviour but there can be other humiliations in the aftermath. Consider the patient of mine who was exposed in the press and had to endure months of profound shame as a consequence. He was on the front page of the tabloids for three weeks. He lost a high-profile position. Another man was also exposed in the press and he lost his marriage because of the fall-out. If you have any high-profile position, I am afraid that you are at the mercy of the press. One footballer could not even come into treatment because he was so fearful of potential press exposure. Another man, who liked a bit of BDSM, had to pull back sharply from this behaviour with dominatrices. His wife found out and, while she was understanding, she realised that he could easily be exposed to the press with overwhelming consequences for his standing in the community.

In the treatment groups that we run, almost half the men are with us because they fear the loss of their relationship and, subsequently, the loss of care of their children. Wives and partners are horribly affected by the discovery of sexually compulsive behaviour. They feel betrayed, cheated, rejected and unattractive. The discovery of the behaviour creates months, even years, of unhappiness. The partners are like people climbing out of a traffic accident. The person that they had thought was a 'safe haven' has turned out not to be. Trust is destroyed. Men can compartmentalise, but women generally do not do this; they see things as a whole, an organic unity.

There can also be consequences for your health and the health of your partner. Suppose you act out with sex workers, and after a couple of drinks, you are a bit careless about the condoms. Oral sex exposes you to herpes and to genital warts. You could subsequently be exposing yourself, and probably your partner, to a sexually transmitted infection. Imagine having to go to the STI clinic with your partner for her to be tested because of your sexually compulsive behaviour. The shame of this would be all-encompassing. One patient who I saw had actually become HIV positive through involvement with a transsexual sex worker in Italy. This poor man also had a wife and two children.

Even if you are not at real risk of a sexually transmitted infection, some men in treatment have health anxiety. They become plagued by fears of HIV/AIDS, even when these fears are entirely irrational. I have seen several men in treatment go through the agonies of fear and uncertainty. One man would be plagued by fears of infection even if he was only masturbated by a sex worker. Another man would also go into a state of acute anxiety, even though he and the woman had never even touched; he had only watched her masturbate.

For most men, the potential consequences are not of the magnitude of those mentioned above. However, there can be implications for your working life. The impact on your professional career is not always easy to see. If there is a heavy addiction to sex or internet sex, the consequences can be cumulative. Let me give you an example: Paul was seen by a colleague looking at internet pornography on his work computer. She did not report this to his employers, but the fear of the loss of his job ruined his Christmas holiday. We called it the 'dark night of the soul' and it was the turning point in his search for recovery. He made an excellent recovery and is now a stalwart in our ongoing aftercare programme.

Sex addiction can also impact on family life. Suppose you are so preoccupied by the desire to act out on the internet that you lose sexual interest in your wife. How does that make her feel? It might have a knock-on effect on your parenting. One patient who came to us had become very aware that he was neglecting to help his children with their homework. Since he came into recovery, his home life has improved and his children are happier.

There can be financial losses as well. One man, a young teacher, had borrowed over £7,000 from payday lenders to finance his sexually compulsive behaviour. If you add up the amount of money spent on sex workers (don't forget the gifts, taxis and hotels), you may well be astonished at the lifetime costs. If you watch free internet porn, the financial costs will not be very high, but if you go onto paid sites, especially live sites, they can escalate rapidly. One rich man paid a sex worker a retainer of £10,000 per month for 20 years. Although he was extremely rich, this would still be, by anybody's reckoning, a great deal of money to pay for sexual services.

There are two overriding problems with sexually compulsive behaviour: it makes you feel shameful and it wastes a great deal of time.

The shame that you feel might be about the double life. It might be about the loss of sexual interest in your partner. It might be the conflict within your personal value system. Participants in our treatment programme tell me that the biggest loss to them is the amount of time wasted on sexual pursuits.

Focusing our minds on the harmful consequences of addictive sexual behaviour is likely to generate shame and weaken an already fragile sense of self. However, it has to be done. There is no point to denial. We need to be fully aware of the consequences of the behaviour. Thinking about the real and potential harmful consequences might strengthen our resolve to make the necessary changes. Let us keep in mind that sexual addiction is a short-term, powerfully rewarded behaviour which can create many long-term losses. The problem is that the reward is so powerful that its strength eclipses the after-effects of the behaviour. If you factor in the fact that we are biologically programmed to be sexual and that the brain chemistry of arousal shuts down cognitive function, you will see that this is a hard one to manage. It can be done, but not easily, and not without perseverance and determination.

The content of this part of the recovery programme has not been easy. While it is important that you have a good look at the harmful consequences of your behaviour, try not to bury yourself under a mountain of shame. If you get too caught up in the shame of the behaviour, it might make you susceptible to further acting out. Sexual behaviour is an escape from shame but the problem is that the means of the escape actually generates higher levels of shame. This creates a vortex taking you into further sexually compulsive behaviour. You need to be realistic but, at the same time, recognise that you are trying to do something about it. There is hope and dignity in that choice.

Exercises

There are two exercises for this week. The first is to make a list of all the harmful consequences of the behaviour over your lifespan. The second is to write out a 'worst case' scenario.

Exercise 1: list of harmful consequences

To help you with the first exercise, I have listed some of the harmful consequences of the behaviour. Read through these, then try to write out the total cost of your own addiction. Include the potential future costs that you are likely to incur if you do not get this sorted.

Financial:

- costs of websites and webcams;
- taking people to dinner, gifts of money or presents;
- subscription costs for an extra telephone;
- lost opportunities at work and therefore a lesser salary;
- entertainment and alcohol costs in the pursuit of sexual adventure;
- payments made to sex workers;
- gifts to extramarital sexual partners;
- being a victim of theft.

Health:

- risk of body lice;
- HIV exposure;
- other sexually transmitted infections;
- lost personal development;
- damaged self-image;
- activation of health anxiety.

Relationships:

- serious impact on your partner;
- your partner leaves you;
- divorce;
- your behaviour is cited as part of the divorce proceedings;
- disinterest in general friendships;
- impaired parenting;
- your partner is driven to despair by your behaviour and self-harm.

Self-image:

- you feel guilty a lot of the time;
- you experience yourself as bad or unworthy;
- you contemplate suicide as a way out;
- you are uncomfortably aware of the contradiction between your behaviour and your values.

Legal and social:

- you are picked up for kerb crawling;
- you are afraid that you will end up in the papers;
- you fear that you will lose your position in society;

- you lose the respect of others;
- lawsuits and divorce are made more difficult;
- you are arrested for downloading illegal pornography;
- you are seen by respected others loitering in a public lavatory.

Physical:

- you are robbed while acting out;
- you are threatened with physical harm while acting out;
- you go to dangerous places in the middle of the night;
- you start using harmful, and probably illegal, substances with sex workers.

Your personal harmful consequences list

Financial

_____

_____

_____

_____

_____

Health

_____

_____

_____

_____

_____

Relationships

_____

_____

_____

_____

_____

Self-image

_____

_____

_____

_____

_____

Legal and social

_____

_____

_____

_____

_____

Physical

_____

_____

_____

_____

_____

Once you have made the list, circle the most significant harmful consequences for you.

Exercise 2: worst case scenario

Write out a 'worst case scenario'. In other words, write out the worst that can happen if you do not change your behaviour.

Here is an example: I will go through all the stress of the break-up of my marriage. This will be followed by a long and protracted divorce, which will cost me a great deal of money and half of all that I have, not to mention ongoing payments. I will have difficulty seeing the children. My partner will marry again and the children will then have a stepdad. I will be sidelined further. My sexual patterns will come out in court and become public knowledge. I will then be alone.

I have known cases exactly like the one above. The partner in this particular case used her husband's involvement with internet pornography as a reason for why she thought he was a threat to his daughters. The divorce proceedings took two years and cost £2 million.

Here is another example: eventually the police will get wind of the fact that I sometimes access sites where the participants are underage. Underage people are not my interest but they are now on my computer. The police arrive and I am arrested. Social Services become involved. The police notify my employers. I lose my job and my wife leaves me in disgust.

I have known not one but many cases where this happened. In one case, the partner was so upset by her husband's use of internet pornography that she called the police and he was arrested for illegal pornography. The case was withdrawn because there was in fact no illegal pornography on his computer. However, Social Services were involved and he was almost barred from the family home.

One final example: one patient of mine was exposed in the press and had to resign from his job. His wife left him and his children were furious. They, too, washed their hands of him. The family disintegrated. He was disconsolate. The disconsolation was made worse by the fact that he had brought it on himself.

Now note down your own worst case scenario:

_____

_____

_____

_____

_____

_____

_____

_____

_____

Recap of tasks for week 3

- Make a Harmful Consequences list.
- Write out a Worst Case Scenario.
- Continue to keep the urge diary.
- Recite Pillar 3 three times a day.

Pillar for week 3

Sometimes my past behaviour has created trouble. When I think about the future possibilities of the behaviour, I get upset. I realise that without this recovery programme, I am opening myself and others to potential unhappiness. The major problem is the impact that this behaviour has on my sense of self. While it is exciting in the short term, I realise that in the long term, I am heading down a destructive path. Today, I redouble my efforts to find recovery and to leave behind unwanted and destructive patterns of sexual behaviour. Today, with a fresh vision of the problems and dangers associated with the behaviour, I am going to press ahead with my recovery towards a way of life that makes me feel good. I will end the double life. This is my resolve for today and for the future, to continue to work for a full recovery from compulsive sexual behaviour.

This week's learning summary:

_____

_____

_____

_____

_____

_____

_____

_____

_____

_____

Provisional sex plan

The function of this chapter of the recovery programme is to get you to actually think about which sexual patterns you find acceptable and which ones you want to leave behind. We are going to do this by preparing a 'sex plan'. In the sex plan, you will be asked to divide your sexual behaviours into three categories: 'OK', 'iffy' and 'not OK'. Behaviours that seem acceptable to you will be included in the 'OK' category. Sexual behaviours that you want to leave behind will be placed in the 'not OK' category, while the 'iffy' category will contain behaviours that you are not yet certain about. The sex plan is provisional and may need to be modified with time and experience.

Your sex plan will be different depending on your circumstances and your world view. Most men in a committed relationship who have made promises of fidelity will choose not to be sexual with another person. They will put sex with other people in the 'not OK' category and sex with the partner in the 'OK' category. Men who are not in a committed relationship will have to consider more closely what they would regard as a responsible pattern of sexual behaviour. What about being sexual with various women whom you are dating? Some men would see this as entirely acceptable and put no boundaries around this chosen behaviour. I would probably recommend not falling into bed with someone on the first date. You will need to be able to remember her name the next morning. I sometimes suggest the three-date rule. This is a simple rule not to have sex with someone until you have been on three dates. This provides a simple boundary between unbridled sexual appetite and human connectedness. It is good practice in the art of sexual containment.

When you prepare your sex plan, you also need to think about masturbation. For most men, it is an occasional to frequent behaviour. This is particularly true where there are major differences in the levels of libido between the man and his partner. I suspect that most men use masturbation to fill in the gaps between sexual opportunities with their partner. Most men would put masturbation in their 'OK' category. I have never understood why we take the view that partnered sex is better than solo sex. I think they are different experiences, but I cannot see why one is deemed to be better than the other. For some men, masturbation is the first step that leads them to full acting out. In this case, they would tend to put masturbation in the 'not OK' or 'iffy' category. However, this is not very common. Generally speaking, most men see masturbation as an acceptable sexual practice alongside partnered sex.

This has not always been the case, as can be illustrated by an interesting aside from American history: John Harvey Kellogg was the medical doctor who invented Kellogg's Cornflakes in 1878. He believed that a bland diet would decrease sexual excitement. He viewed sexual excitement as a bad thing, seeing masturbation, in particular, as a terrible vice that led to all kinds of serious medical complaints and conditions. He invented Cornflakes as an antidote, in part, to masturbation. Remember that the next time you have breakfast.

I have had a number of men in our treatment programme who put masturbation in the 'not OK' category because they had adopted a religious commitment that was demanding, and masturbation conflicted with their firmly held religious views. I have a patient who was raised in East Africa and there were major social restrictions placed upon masturbation. Those of you who were raised in conservative or highly religious environments may also have reservations about masturbation. The same was generally true in western culture until fairly recently. These taboos and prohibitions still linger on. The term 'wanker' is still used as a term of mild abuse. This indicates that masturbation still occupies a somewhat ambiguous place in modern society. I would suggest that you think about masturbation carefully and decide where you want to put it on your sex plan.

When preparing your sex plan, you will also have to think about how you view masturbation with the use of accompanying erotic imagery. Some people would put masturbation to internet pornography into their 'OK' category. I had one middle-aged patient who chose to use internet pornography as his sexual outlet. His wife did not want to be sexual with him at all. He did not want to use sex workers so he deliberately, and with reflection, decided that the internet would have to serve as his sexual outlet. Other people might feel that the use of internet pornography is unacceptable. This might be because they have already identified that the use of internet pornography is, for them, a slippery slope into other unwanted behaviours. Although I will go into this in greater detail in the chapter on the internet towards the end of this book, habitual use of internet pornography can lead to, or accompany, increased isolation. Sometimes you can get so used to looking at endless images of big-busted women gagging for casual sex that you can begin to think real women are, or should be, like that. This is rarely true and the internet can distort your picture of a naked woman. The exaggerated features and behaviours of women on the internet can reduce the sex appeal of a real naked woman. As we saw in the chapter on supernormal stimuli, we come to prefer the exaggerated over the natural.

If you have made use of sex workers in the past, you will need to decide where to place this activity within your sex plan. We find in our treatment programme that men who have been accustomed to using the services of sex workers, and chose to place this in the 'not OK' category on their sex plan, can stop that behaviour relatively easily. This is because the use of a sex worker involves searching the internet, making a phone call, getting money from the cash point, driving to an address, finding a parking place, finding the flat and then going up the stairs. This process provides many exit points and opportunities to think of the negative outcome and to change your mind. Internet sexual behaviour is much more difficult to leave behind. This is simply because it is so easy. In the blink of an eye, you can be transported from the humdrum of everyday life into the pleasure of sexual oblivion. It just takes an instant and a couple of clicks of the mouse. The process is so quick that it does not allow much time for an argument between the part of you that wants to do this and the part of you that does not.

The choices that you make about your sex plan will also be determined by age. In our society, there is a deeply held view that it is not appropriate to want to be sexual if you are old. There is little provision made in residential homes for the possibility of sexual behaviour. While the sex drive diminishes with age, there is no reason why you should be denied sexual pleasure just because you have turned 65. I had a clergyman who came to me because he thought he was using too much internet pornography. He was 85 and lived in an all-male residential community. It seemed to me that he was making the best of a bad job. Because I was concerned that he was becoming isolated on the computer, I suggested that he might try to increase his social contacts and not worry too much about his use of internet pornography.

It can also be extremely difficult to have any kind of sexual experience if you are disabled. Care assistants are not allowed to help. You are not able to get out. This often leaves a dilemma about sexual options.

There are particular issues that should be considered if you are a gay man reading this book. Gay sexuality has a distinctive character that needs to be factored into your thinking. It is said that gay men are more sexually active than straight men. This is not because they are gay but because they are men. Research shows that gay men have higher levels of addiction than the rest of the population but this is not about a lifestyle choice. It is because gay men, on the whole, belong to a stigmatised minority and the higher levels of addiction are a response to stigmatisation. If you are gay and are not in a committed relationship, the same advice applies to you as to straight single men. Try to wait for a few dates before jumping into bed with someone. If you are in an open relationship, the same advice also applies. The issue is the same for straight and gay alike: if your sexual patterns are out of control, bring harmful consequences and are used to anaesthetise some negative feeling state, then there is a probability that you are sexually compulsive.

I remember the joke, 'It's been so long since I have had sex, that I've forgotten who gets tied up'. If your sexual repertory involves something 'quirky' like bondage and submission, being tied up or tying up, cross-dressing or water-sports, do not get into a funk about it. Research shows that people with quirky behaviours have the same psychological health as the rest of the population. People can feel very ashamed about having a quirk and if you are one of those, let me try to reassure you. You did not ask for it and you are not responsible for having it. You are only responsible for how you manage it. You can find more information about this in the chapter on 'paraphila' towards the end of this book.

Sexual behaviour comes in all sizes and shapes and is generally the product of childhood development. Authorities tell us that male sexual templates (built-in sexual preferences) are fixed in place between the ages of seven and nine years old. Other authorities take the view that sexual templates are formed between four and eleven years old, with a bell-shaped curve which places the peak age of development approximately between seven and nine years old. Sexual templates are then activated at adolescence. Some researchers suggest that final changes can be made to the template at this time. For the most part, we seem to be stuck with our sexual scripts and they do not change much over the life span. These templates operate automatically and are not deliberately chosen preferences.

The disgust response is also set up in early childhood. This too operates largely without choice. One person can find some sexual behaviour to be the apex of their sexual yearning while another person might find the activity to be outrageously disgusting. Take heterosexual anal sex as an example. One participant might think it is the best sexual activity known to humankind, while another person, often the female partner, might be totally disgusted with the idea. The disgust response can be activated because the sexual organs have a dual role: evacuation as well as conjugal connection. In a couple relationship, these differences of preference need to be negotiated with consideration and respect. Both parties in the couple relationship need to give and take. However, most of us would not be willing to pressure our partners into a pattern of sexual behaviour in which they were most unwilling to participate. At the same time, the more adventurous of the partners should not be made to feel like a pervert because he suggests something different to the sexual expectations of the other. Having a full and frank discussion about such issues can prevent a great deal of long-term heartache.

I have written that the sexual templates that operate in our minds are largely fixed. Some authorities would question this. The internet, for example, might be able to change some of the templates. You might get bored with watching heterosexual couples having sex and so you have a look around for greater variety and go on to bondage. This looks interesting and novel. The idea is that by looking at these new sites, you get bonded to them by the pleasure of an orgasm. Some people think that this can happen through your neurochemistry. The brain releases oxytocin during orgasm, and oxytocin is the brain chemistry of bonding so, in effect, you become bonded to the image on the screen. My own view is that the internet can bring a latent sexual script to the forefront of the mind by its continued use. It is not so much the creation of a new script but the resurgence of a buried script. It is easy to begin to accustom yourself to different sexual scenarios by their use in masturbation. I suspect that something like this happens with men who like young women. Who does not? But the age can creep down and before you know it, you are looking at the barely legal and then problems arise. If your sexual interest includes a sexual attraction to underage people or involves coercion, the only answer is not to do it. In such cases, I would suggest that you seek professional help. This subject is beyond the scope of this book but if you pursue these sexual interests, you would be involving yourself in a grave offence. Even graver is the harm that would be caused to another person.

The sex plan that you produce will be provisional, as you will need to try it out and see whether it works. It might be modified with time and experience. All you have to do is to think about your sexual patterns and consider which ones you want to leave behind and which ones are acceptable to you. In the outer box, you write down the sexual behaviours that you feel are 'not OK' for you to do. In the inner box you write the ones that are 'OK' for you. In the middle box, you put the questionable and uncertain behaviours. The function of this process is to get you to think about what you are doing and come up with a considered action plan for what you want.

I have taken a couple of real examples from people in our treatment programme for you to have a look at.

Wayne:

NOT OK: sex with sex workers
OK: sex with the wife and masturbation
IFFY: cruising websites of women offering sexual services

He put the cruising of websites of women offering sexual services in the 'iffy' box because he was aware that this has historically prompted him to make the phone call and eventually see the sex worker. It seemed better to stop the process before the arousal chemistry could take hold and move him into the 'bubble' where he would lose control.

Roger:

NOT OK: saunas or sex parties, internet pornography and drugs of abuse
OK: sex with his partner
IFFY: alcohol

Roger was a gay man who had a history of continuous sex from Thursday to Sunday, using a variety of recreational drugs to maintain the process. He would start off with the drugs and spend the next three days going from sauna to sauna and from sex party to sex party. He had been doing this for seven years. In the past he had acted in pornographic movies. Alcohol was in the 'iffy' box because Roger was aware that alcohol lowered his inhibitions and made him vulnerable to dangerous sexual behaviour. Roger did well and stopped completely. We celebrated the first anniversary of his sobriety with cake and ice cream.

Exercise: provisional sex plan

It is now time for you to make your provisional sex plan. I call it 'provisional' because it needs to tried and tested for usefulness. With experience it can be altered. In the inner box write the behaviours that seem acceptable to you. In the outer box, list the sexual behaviours that you want to leave behind. In the middle box, write down behaviours that you are not yet certain about. Keep in mind that this is a provisional sex plan. It can be amended. Try to be realistic about it and do not fall into one extreme or the other, putting too much or too little in the 'not OK' box. Just try to be realistic.

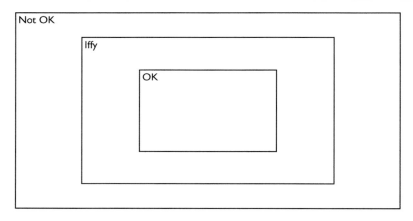

Figure 2.4.1 Provisional sex plan.

Recap of tasks for week 4

* Make a provisional sex plan.
* Continue to keep the urge diary.
* Recite Pillar 4 three times a day.

Pillar for week 4

I am aware that some of my sexual patterns are not helpful. I intend to consider the whole range of my sexual behaviours and make the necessary changes. This will be hard at first but these changes will become easier with time. I will take it a day at a time. I will change my behaviour. I will leave behind damaging and destructive behaviour and I will embrace sexual patterns that leave me feeling good when the sexual act is over. With determination, resolve and commitment, I will change. The change has already started, perhaps imperceptibly, but it has started. It will gather momentum as I go through this recovery programme.

This week's learning summary:

_____

_____

_____

_____

Family of origin

Addictive processes seem to evolve in our lives and then take on a life of their own. They operate until we come to a point that we get so sick and tired that we decide to do something about them. This is the point that you have come to and you have decided to take some action to change the situation.

The purpose of this section is to come to a better understanding about how your addictive processes came into being. No one asks for a pattern of sexual behaviour that is painful and destructive in the aftermath. We do not go out shopping for a pattern of sexual behaviour that will cause us to feel bad or which might be destructive to others.

In fact, addictive patterns evolve from our family of origin. The emergence of addictive sexuality has its origins in childhood and in matters that were beyond our control. If you are a sex addict or have a quirky sexual behaviour, be assured that you did not ask for it. Of course, you are responsible for the way you deal with it. You are responsible for your actions and for their consequences but you are not responsible, in the first place, for their presence in your life.

There is always a debate over whether addictive behaviour is determined by genetics or by environment. As I have noted before, a number of researchers would maintain that about 50 per cent of the tendency to addiction is genetic. Bear in mind that they are not saying that addiction is genetic but rather that a *predisposition* towards addiction is genetic. I take the view that it is the family environment that is important for determining whether the tendency towards addiction will turn into the reality of an addiction.

There is a French proverb which says, 'The child is the father of the man'. It succinctly captures the fact that events that happen in childhood have long-term consequences. Negative childhood events that can have a profound impact upon us include abuse, continual criticism, a withholding mother and the absence of proper nurture, as well as events that were belittling or shaming. Negative events imprint on the brain differently from positive events. Negative events constitute threat and our brains are sensitive to threat. They are designed that way because threats are dangerous and the emotions associated with them trigger action. Take, for example, fear. We have fear to protect us from danger. We either flee, we fight or we are paralysed. The last of these options is the equivalent of playing dead, the final desperate mechanism to avoid being harmed. The foundation events that shaped your sexual patterns probably took place before you had any real memory, but a part of you does remember nevertheless. The responses are encoded in your behaviour, even if not in your conscious memory.

Sexual behaviour is part of an in-built drive. We are biologically programmed to be sexual on a regular basis. Sexual behaviour is not like the learned use of alcohol or recreational drugs. The body chemistry is within you and not outside of you. Some of us learn to escape negative feeling states by the use of alcohol, while some of us learn to use behaviours which generate their own rewards as a way of escaping negative feeling states. I know that if I take physical exercise in the morning, I will feel well and have a better day than if I lie in bed and eat a cooked breakfast. I have learned that the repetitious use of my muscles in aerobic and anaerobic exercise changes my feeling states. If I am feeling bad, I know that there is something that I can do that will change that feeling state. Of course, exercise is also good for me and keeps my weight down; not being overweight is also good for me. On the other hand, if I am feeling bad and escape into internet pornography, I have nothing to show for it except wasted time. Instead of wanting things that will bring quality to life and long-term wellbeing, the sex addict chooses short-term escape. This escape can bring with it many problems.

All sex addicts have experienced some kind of painful background. If we understand our past experiences, we have the opportunity to break free from them and to make fresh choices for the future. We need to be able to identify the problems in the past that gave rise to our present behaviour. Many of us deny that anything bad ever happened to us. The point is not to blame your parents but just to try to understand the way your behaviour was created in the family of origin. Our parents usually did the best job they knew how. They are not to blame; after all, they are just someone else's children acting out unconscious internalised rules and mechanisms in their adult lives, just as you do.

Sometimes the damage is easy to understand. If your mother or father was an alcoholic, you will be able to see immediately that the alcoholic has only one dominating relationship and that is with alcohol. If either of your parents was depressed or suffered from a mental illness, through no fault of their own they would probably not have been able to parent you properly. Sometimes children are parented not for the needs and requirements of the child but to meet the needs of the parent. This is subtle and might seem hard to recognise. Less subtly, I have had a lot of patients that were regularly beaten as children. In one case, the mother broke a tennis racket over her son's back. In another, the child was beaten with his mother's high heel shoe and was left with cuts on his head. I know that child-rearing practices differ from culture to culture and from age to age, but it would be hard to describe breaking a tennis racket over a child's back as anything less than child abuse. One child was made to go outside and choose a switch with which to be spanked. Another child, from a 'good home', was left on the doorstep naked in winter. These practices may seem outrageous but they come from the routine stories of the sex addicts who come to see me and enter our recovery programme.

Addictions rarely present alone; they tend to occur in combination with other addictions. It is rare for a man just to be a sex addict. A frequent combination is alcohol and sex. The alcohol disinhibits and opens the doors for unbridled sexual behaviour. One patient only ever smoked when he was acting out sexually. He had combined nicotine and sex as an addictive combination. He took this further because he only looked at pictures of women smoking. Another combination seen frequently at our clinic is sex and work. As we saw earlier, they form a cycle of control and release. Work is the control part of the cycle; the control of work is followed by the release of sexual acting out. Sometimes the combination is sex and religion. Religion is pursued for the good feelings that it generates and sexual behaviour for the same reasons. With this combination, high levels of shame and remorse come together because one behaviour is so antithetical to the other. We will look more at the topic of multiple addictions in the chapter on cross addictions and comorbid disorders towards the end of this book.

Let's take a look at the childhood backgrounds of some of the men who have been my patients. All these men have a sexual addiction and some of them also have a quirky sexual interest. These examples are taken from my book *CBT for Compulsive Sexual Behaviour – A Guide for Professionals* and a fuller account of their acting out patterns can be found in the section on Case Studies in that book.

Let us turn first to Robin. Robin was raised in a highly sexualised family atmosphere. His parents were committed to one another but this commitment seemed to exclude Robin from being noticed as a child. He was aware of sex parties in the house, although he was never exposed to them directly. His parents' exclusive relationship meant that he was never seen and, as an adult, this manifested into the sexual quirk of repeated exhibitionism. Robin needed to be noticed and valued as a man and this gave rise to exposing his erect penis to women on buses and trains.

Thomas was actively disliked by his father. His mother was so preoccupied by her own needs that she had no time for him or interest in him. Furthermore, Thomas was a self-hating gay man. Gay men often internalise the wider societal view that they are defective. This happened to Thomas and he escaped into internet pornography.

Francois was born a 'blue baby'. His father was always absent. He began using pornography when he was very young. He would 'borrow' his father's pornography collection. He experienced three occasions that we might describe as sexual abuse, the first when he was four years old. It was recalled in fragmentary memory. As an adult, he was sexually compulsive with countless women.

With Matthew, the trauma began even before he was born. His mother's parents wanted him aborted. He now speaks with disgust about his parents who rely upon him for their income. He became addicted to making money, as well as going to sex clubs and sex parties. This was alongside his marriage.

Mason was put up for adoption. The effect of this was a lifelong experience of not being wanted. He went to live with a grandmother but was taken into care when the social workers found that the grandmother was negligent in her care of him. Eventually he was adopted by a dysfunctional family and raised in that family. He went on to use sex workers.

Henry was raised in a family without boundaries. He can remember his father having loud sex with his wife in the caravan they used for their holidays. Henry went on to be sexual with both his stepsisters and went to prison for having sex with a minor. In that family, there were no boundaries.

Some of us will have had similar experiences to these men, while some of us will not. In my own case, the problem was not abuse but rather neglect. At least, if you are hit, it means that you are important, even if for the wrong reasons. Neglect can be worse. If you are neglected, then you are not important to anyone. After all these years, I still crave milk before going to bed. If I do not have milk, I become alarmed. Even if I do not remember in my thinking brain that I was neglected, my body remembers and has not forgotten.

As we can see from the examples given above, many sexually addicted men have traumatic birth stories. There may have been traumatic incidents during their mother's pregnancy. Research tells us that the unborn child is sensitive to events even while in their mother's womb. For example, unborn children like Mozart but not Wagner. How sensible. The unborn child can detect the presence of his father. Stephen Verny, a paediatrician, writes in *The Secret Life of the Unborn Child* (1981) that children born by caesarean section experience more sexual problems in adult life than children who are born naturally. He gives no references to substantiate this view.

Sometimes the problems that give rise to sexual addiction lie with nobody. Some men with a physical abnormality feel inferior to others. Others may experience difficulties as a result of the environment in which they grew up. I had one patient who was traumatised by his mother teaching him how to sew up flesh wounds when he was seven years old. He and his family lived in a place of war and his mother, a GP, was anxious that he could do this in case one of the family was hurt in a bombing raid. There were bombs going off all around them. This demonstrates how the origins of addiction do not always lie in the wilfulness of others but can emerge from situations completely out of anyone's control.

The most frequent combination of factors in the family of origin that I see in clinical practice is the combination of a distant, critical father and a cold, withdrawn, non-demonstrative mother. One patient had such a mother and his sexual fantasy was to be massaged by a group of naked women, their breasts hanging over him. Take the sex out of the fantasy and its meaning becomes clear. The patient was trying to move from maternal destitution to female plenitude. The fantasy was simply a reversal of the reality of his early life. Maternal deprivation is the term that I give to situations where the mother is unable or unwilling to consistently engage with the child. The child gets the message that he is the problem.

It is now right to get a bit technical about the precursors for addiction. The hypothesis is that when children have sub-optimal care, they never learn to manage their internal emotions, or feeling states. The ability to manage feeling states is downloaded from the primary caregivers to the child. Children learn to regulate their internal states from the regulation that they receive from their caregivers. You can see this daily on the streets. Over and over, I see mothers regulating the body temperature of their children by adjusting coats and scarves. The same thing happens with other feeling states, such as loneliness, shame, regret, anger and fear. We learn to regulate by being regulated, and we internalise this process. Children who have never learned this from their parents are the ones who turn to substances and behaviours to regulate their emotional life. After all, if you are feeling anxious or shameful, a couple of glasses of wine or a couple of hours on the internet relieves the feeling state by providing a means of temporary escape. Addiction is a learned activity for the management of negative feeling states. The problem is that the solution is not without its concomitant problems. You feel shame and therefore you act out with sex workers, but this causes you to feel more shame and so an endless repetitive cycle is created. This pattern is never-ending, until you get so fed up with it that there is no alternative except to pursue recovery.

Of course there are many addictive substances and many addictive repetitious activities. Eating can be an escape, sex can be a place of oblivion and recreational drugs can provide missing excitement. You can lose yourself in work or ecstatic religion. It is perhaps interesting to think about why a person ends up addicted to sex, rather than another major addictive behaviour. The only expert who has tackled this question is Aviel Goodman, the author of *Sexual Addiction, An Integrated Approach* (1998). He hypothesises that sexual addiction emerges as a primary escape mechanism in family environments which he describes as 'sexualised'. This sexualisation can be covert or overt. A sex negative family can be just as obsessed by sex as a sex positive family. These may seem to be two ends of the spectrum but they actually amount to the same thing. Both are preoccupations with sex. One is expressed as continually talking about it and the other as never mentioning it.

Exercises

You can choose to do either the trauma egg or shame museum exercise this week, or even both. They amount to the same exercise. Both are an investigation into the less happy aspects of childhood. Bear in mind that sexual addiction is a behaviour that is used to anaesthetise feeling states that are difficult to manage. These states were set up in childhood, but they need not prevail in adult life.

Exercise 1: trauma egg

This week's exercise is designed to help you uncover and reflect upon negative events in your childhood. We all have them, no matter how warm and friendly our family environment was.

Take a large sheet of paper, preferably A1, and draw a large egg shape. Inside the egg you are going to draw pictures that represent experiences that you have had in life that are shaming or non-nurturing, possibly even abusive. It is important to draw the representation and not write it out, as this makes use of a different part of the brain. This is not an art competition and some of you might already being saying to yourselves, 'But, I can't draw'. That is probably your critical voice in operation. I am just asking you to draw a representation of the experience, not a Rembrandt. The important thing is not to create something that someone else will say is good but instead to draw a representation of the event and possibly the feelings that went with it. It is called an egg because the current behaviours are born from the experiences inside it. Start with age zero and go up to your current age. Sometimes it is even possible to go back before birth. So start at the beginning, at the time of your birth, or before, and draw out all the incidents that you know about that were shaming, abusive, harmful or non-nurturing. I have included an example, with the patient's kind permission.

The source of your sexual addiction probably lies in the events recounted in the trauma egg, so it would be particularly helpful if you were able to go through the trauma egg with a friend or another trustworthy person. You could do this with your partner, although she may be too traumatised by your sexual acting out to be the right person. If you are in individual therapy, the therapist would be an ideal person to hear your story.

Exercise 2: shame museum

Another way of doing this exercise is the shame museum. In this exercise, you draw each experience on a single sheet of A4 paper. On another sheet of A4 you write out the experience as far as you are able to remember it. All the sheets and their corresponding descriptions are then bound together into a Guide Book to the Shame Museum.

When my client Patrick completed the shame museum exercise, he drew a picture of himself sitting in the back of the car being driven off to boarding school. The face on the child is clearly frightened. You do not have to be an art critic to recognise the fear. The parents are sitting in the front looking straight ahead. Patrick is alone and isolated in the back of the car. The commentary that goes with it was:

> I am sitting in the back of the car being driven away from all my friends and all that is familiar to me. I feel a lot of fear. I feel like I have done something wrong. I feel like a convicted criminal being sent to prison or one of those people during the terror in France being taken for execution. I am totally alone. The feeling of helplessness and punishment is overwhelming. I feel wretched. I feel guilty. I feel a failure.

It does not take a lot of awareness to understand that Patrick acts out on fear and isolation. In the scenario he describes, it is possible to see the

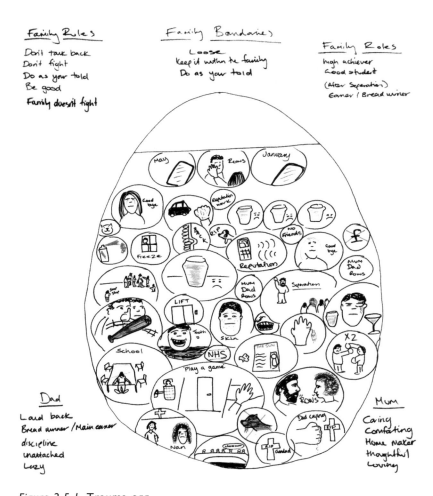

Figure 2.5.1 Trauma egg.

Source: Reproduced by kind permission of the patient.

antecedents of the adult behaviour. Patrick lives in a state of fear and this fear was set up in the event above. Of course, the picture was of the defining event but the reality was that he probably lived thorough many such experiences of fear, shame, guilt and isolation. These feeling states were intolerable and he escaped from them through the use of internet pornography.

Recap of tasks for week 5

- Draw your trauma egg and/or make your guide to the shame museum.
- Continue to keep the urge diary.
- Read Pillar 5 three times a day.

Pillar for week 5

My addiction started a long time ago. It was probably accidently set up in my childhood. It has operated in my adult life to help me manage shame, anxiety and loneliness. I have used it to provide excitement when things were boring. I have used it to fill my free time when I could have been doing more productive things. I have used it to escape distress. But all of these things are just escapes. They do nothing to actually change anything apart from provide short-term avoidance of the implications of the things that I am escaping. The behaviour has solved nothing. Now I am determined to make a change. I am determined to learn to live with painful feelings. I am determined to find healthy ways to manage these difficult and distressing states. I will continue and I will eventually triumph. I will leave behind these sexual patterns that create confusion and damage and I will embrace a way of being sexual that gives me pleasure in the short term and joy in the long run.

This week's learning summary:

_____

_____

_____

_____

_____

_____

_____

_____

_____

_____

Week 6

Cycle of addiction

Introduction

The aim of this chapter is to help you analyse the steps involved in your own sexual acting out and to bring them into conscious awareness. We can describe the sequence of events involved in acting out as a 'cycle of addiction'. It is called a cycle because it is self-reinforcing, and we go round

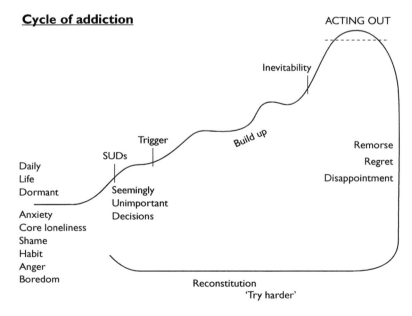

Figure 2.6.1 Generic cycle of addiction.

Source: Roughly adapted by Thaddeus Birchard from Bays and Freeman-Longo 1989.

and round it time and again. Unless your cycle of addiction is understood, it will be difficult to break. Once it is understood, you will be able to take corrective action. We can depict the cycle of addiction in terms of a diagram.

In this chapter, we will begin to look at each of the components that make up this cycle. Men in our treatment programme describe the cycle of addiction as the most important intervention to help them leave behind unwanted sexual behaviour. Let us begin with the dormant phase.

Dormant phase

In the dormant phase, it probably seems as though life is just ticking along as usual. Things are going well, and it may appear as though the addiction is not present. You may convince yourself that you do not have a problem. However, it does not take much for the cycle to be triggered, as your sexual acting out is the only way that you have developed to deal with difficult thoughts, feelings and negative events.

Precursors

There are three prior components to acting out: the negative feeling states, seemingly unimportant decisions and the triggers that set in motion the addictive cycle. The cycle normally begins with experiencing negative feelings. We refer to these internal feeling states as 'precursors' to the sexual acting out. As we saw in Chapter 2, the primary feeling states that give rise to sexual acting out are depression, loneliness, anxiety, boredom and shame. These feelings are experienced as intolerable, and sexual behaviour is used as a way to escape from the feelings and create a temporary relief.

Let us look at an example. Ben was a successful financial wizard. He had started out with a firm of brokers and eventually left them to go into business for himself. He owned a flat in Knightsbridge and a house in France and was extraordinarily well off. He had a wife and one child. I had met the wife and child incidentally at the door of the clinic. She was a good-looking woman and the child was well turned out. But all of his success was built on anxiety that he would fail. He lived day-to-day in states of constant anxiety. The anxiety was relieved by using sex workers. His wife knew nothing of this and thought that their marriage was 'perfect'. Every time there was a crucial meeting scheduled or a risky and uncertain process about to take place, Ben would see sex workers. He also used them as a reward for getting through the difficult and uncertain meetings and work day events. Ben's pattern was to use sex workers when he was anxious and to use them as a reward once the event had passed successfully. Ben did not come into treatment and there was no further information. If he had come into treatment, we would have identified the relationship between anxiety/reward and his use of sex workers and then taught him other anxiety management strategies. Ben was seriously putting his family at risk and jeopardising their welfare and contentment.

The problem with using sexual acting out as a mood-changing strategy is that, whilst it might seem to work in the short term, in the long run it actually makes the situation worse. If you are suffering from low mood, sexual acting out will leave you in a worse mood afterwards. Equally, if you are anxious, you are likely to be even more anxious after acting out. The same applies to shame, boredom and loneliness; these negative feeling states are heightened after acting out. Similarly if there are difficulties with your relationship dynamics, these are likely to worsen as a result of acting out.

For another client, Roderick, the precursor to acting out was feelings of inadequacy. The first part of the pattern for him was the thought 'I might fail'. This caused anxiety. Roderick was a perfectionist and the fear of failure was high. Although he was a high achiever, the achievement was built on the fear of failure. The fear of failure rose out of a belief that he was, in fact, defective. His whole life, in the financial services industry, had been spent going from success to success. In fact, it would be true to say that the fear of failure was the driving force that contributed to his high levels of achievement. Roderick had an important contract to negotiate. The thought went through his head, 'What if I fail?' This thought triggered high levels of anxiety. He escaped the anxiety by visiting a sex worker. From the moment that he began to plan to see the sex worker, he was transported out of anxiety into a place of pleasurable oblivion. It was not just seeing the sex worker that was sexual oblivion but the whole process: searching the internet, reading the profiles, driving to the flat, going up and entering her room. From the beginning of these activities he was in a mood-altered state. He had a double hit. The anxiety was relieved, which was a plus and the sexual excitement was an additional plus. However, the escape did nothing to actually change the underlying belief system that he might fail. He escaped it but it would continue on his return from sexual oblivion. This meant that the underlying causation was never cured. He remained in a permanent state of anxiety about failure and the use of sex workers was the answer. In fact, it was a short-term strategy and, thus, involved a never-ending cycle of sexual behaviour. The sexual behaviour was not actually for sex but it was an escape from the fear of failure.

Let's look at one more example. Jason also acts out by visiting sex workers. The precursor for Jason's acting out is a feeling of low self-worth, bordering upon self-hatred. When Jason is feeling bad about himself, he visits websites dedicated to sex workers providing degrading sexual services. The visits to the websites set in motion a crazy chain of events. He loses all control over his behaviour and relentlessly drives to north London to pay a woman to perform these services. He owes a huge amount of money to payday lenders. He thinks to himself, 'I am shit and I do not deserve anything better'. This plunges him into the pit of shame. For him, the feeling is chronic, constant and unremitting. The problem is that, every time Jason acts out with one of the dominatrices, it confirms his belief that he is worthless. The cycle of addiction therefore continues.

Seemingly unimportant decisions

The next important feature in understanding your cycle of addiction is to learn to recognise the seemingly unimportant decisions that can lead you into sexually compulsive behaviour. For example, let's imagine that you decide to go for a walk. You leave your house and you could turn left or right. If you turn left, you pass a school and a playground. If you have a sexual interest in children, turning left would be a mistake. Turning right would take you towards the shops and then towards a leafy suburban street. Turning left or right seems like a seemingly unimportant decision but it is not unimportant because it has the greater possibility of setting in motion a series of unfortunate events that could be disastrous for another and would have profound consequences for you.

It is important for you to start to recognise the seemingly unimportant decisions that can lead you into sexually compulsive behaviour. For example, your partner is going shopping and you decide to stay at home and relax. However, this 'relaxation time' provides you with an opportunity to act out. Once the arousal chemistry starts to increase, it becomes increasingly difficult to withdraw. Staying at home was a seemingly unimportant decision. Or perhaps your partner goes to bed and you say, 'Darling, I will come up later'. Another opportunity is presented which favours sexually compulsive behaviour. The time that you go to bed is a seemingly unimportant decision that might have important consequences for your sexual sobriety.

I had a patient that used to pick up sex workers when driving home from work. Each day he drove home through the red light district and, time and time again, he would act out. Something as simple and as inconsequential as the way he drove home set in motion his arousal chemistry and took him from a businessman to a sexual predator. I said to him, 'Make a conscious decision to drive home a different way'.

The decision about where to sit on the underground could also set in motion sexual acting out. Do you deliberately choose a position so that you can see and subsequently fantasise about one of the women sitting on the opposite seat? You could actually sit somewhere else. You could move or take out a newspaper. One patient used to pick up women at the airport. He travelled back and forth to India. Just sitting in the Business Lounge was his seemingly unimportant decision. I said, 'Read a book'.

One of the purposes of the cycle of addiction is to help you learn to notice and then to avoid these seemingly unimportant decisions. These decisions take you into triggers and triggers take you into addictive sexual behaviour.

Triggers

Recognising your cycle of addiction helps you to identify the specific triggers for your sexual acting out. The triggers are sometimes also known as cues. One man I worked with was being shown around an empty flat by a woman estate agent and he could feel an increase in arousal. He was aware that he had only been in a flat alone with a woman to have sex. The situation and ambiance were triggers for him. This took him into sexualised conversation which was not reciprocated. Afterwards, he felt like a fool.

For men in relationships, the triggers may be related to unhealthy dynamics hidden within the relationship. The hidden dynamics tend to be an over-controlling partner or a partner who is threatening to abandon him. Take Mary and Joe, a married couple. Mary brought Joe into the clinic for us to 'fix' him. She had become aware of his use of internet pornography and his rather frequent visits to massage parlours for sexual services. She was furious and immediately took the view that this was his problem and he needed to get it fixed. I was aware from the start that Mary had an overwhelming need to control Joe. This became increasingly apparent in the course of the treatment programme. It was clear that Joe was trying to escape from his wife's need to control him, using the internet and sexual services as private 'me time' activities. Many men escape from overcontrolling partners by going into the garden shed or down into the basement, where the tools are kept. The internet can also provide a place to escape from the demands of the partner. Mary wanted to know where Joe was all the time, who he was with and what he was doing. She would ring him at the office 10 times a day to check. Joe found this claustrophobic and intrusive; it acted as a trigger and he used internet pornography to create some private space. The more Mary tried to control Joe, the more he wanted to act out. In working with them as a couple, I noticed that it was hard for Mary to allow herself to let up on Joe. She accused me of blaming her for Joe's internet use. I was not. I was trying to point out that a dynamic had been set up in the relationship: the more she pressured Joe, the more he needed to act out to escape the pressure and the more he acted out, the more she pressured. There were other factors behind Joe's sexual acting out, but this dysfunctional dynamic was helping to create the problems that it was trying to solve.

Build-up

During the build-up phase, you will be taking incremental steps towards sexual acting out. For example, if your sexual acting out involves visiting escorts, during the build-up phase you might look at an escort website, read the profiles, perhaps send an email or call one of the women, just with the aim of gaining information. You may even still be telling yourself that you do not actually intend to act out, but in reality all of these activities are taking you to the point where acting out is inevitable.

During the build-up phase, the arousal chemistry begins to increase in the brain. The prospect of the immediate reward of sexual pleasure is so great that it eclipses any thought of the aftermath. Short-term gain is prioritised over long-term wellbeing.

Point of inevitability

This is the point at which there is no going back, and probably the point at which you finally admit to yourself that you are definitely going to act out. It might be standing on the doorstep of the sex worker's flat ringing the doorbell, picking up the phone and dialling the sex chat number or clicking on the hard-core pornography website.

Acting out

As we have already learned, 'acting out' is the term that we use to describe the sexual behaviour itself. Feelings during the acting out phase may be mixed. On the one hand you may experience the exhilaration that comes from the release from the negative feeling state, as well as the excitement of sexual arousal. However, you may also already begin to experience some negative feelings at this point, as the after-effects sometimes begin to set in before the acting out has even finished.

After-effects

The after-effects of sexual acting out are all too familiar to most of you. These are generally debilitating shame, remorse, self-attack and a plundered sense of self. I have met some men trying to get into recovery, usually at their partner's behest, who do not have these after-effects, but most men do have them. They ask themselves the question, 'How could I have done it again?' The remorse can be overwhelming and the distress far-reaching. Yet despite these feelings, the man has to get on with family life, turn up at work, go out to lunch with friends and put on a 'there is nothing wrong' face to his partner.

The after-effects are often worse when the sexual acting out is discovered by someone else. Let us look at the example of Fin, who both loathed himself and feared adult women. When he drew a trauma egg in therapy, all the adult women included in it were punishing or rejecting. Fin was isolated and friendless. His overriding thought was 'I can never have a girlfriend'. This, combined with the relentless isolation, set in motion the need to escape. Internet pornography was his sole escape. However, he had been arrested once and the arrest was a profound trauma which confirmed and accentuated his isolation and sense of being friendless. He believed he would never be able to have a relationship. This drove him further into internet pornography and the sex addiction cycle continued.

Reconstitution

Sometimes quickly, but more often slowly, the feelings of shame recede and you begin to reconstitute your life. After reconstitution, there is a return to the dormant phase, and as soon as an unbearable negative emotion is experienced, the cycle starts all over again.

Example

I will now take you through the cycle of addiction of a client, Ben, so that you can begin to see how all the elements fit together. Ben worked in the City as a smart, competent executive who ran a number of accounts for important clients. He was tidy and meticulous. He lived in the suburbs with his wife and child. His wife did not work but stayed at home providing full-time child care. Their daughter was three years old.

Ben would go out at lunchtime to buy a newspaper. He would go into the newsagents, where the top shelf would grab his attention. The top shelf contained all the girly magazines. These magazines were not hard-core pornography but were full of nude big-busted women. He would surreptitiously leaf through these magazines. This would then start his cycle of addiction. He would then wander around London looking at the advertisements for sexual services in the phone boxes. After a while, he would start ringing the women offering sexual services. A little later, he would start visiting their locations asking about prices and the services they offered. He would then start taking poppers. Eventually he would come to a decision point and decide to go to one of these women or to a massage parlour. He would be masturbated or given oral sex. After his orgasm, feeling wretched, he would make his way to the train station. The guilt was so great that he would call in at Westminster Cathedral and go to confession before getting his train home. Over the next week or so, he would begin to feel better. He would see me. He would go to a meeting of Sex Addicts Anonymous. He would do extra workouts at the gym. Eventually the shame, remorse and guilt would fade and then about three weeks later he would go out to the newsagent to buy another newspaper. When I knew him, the cycle had been going on for eight years at three-weekly intervals. He had borrowed money from his client accounts to pay for his use of sex workers. This is illegal. He was hopelessly lost in a never-ending cycle of addiction.

Ben's cycle looks like this:

Cycle of addiction

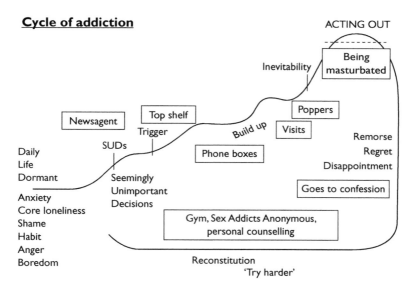

Figure 2.6.2 Ben's cycle of addiction.
Source: Roughly adapted by Thaddeus Birchard from Bays and Freeman-Longo 1989.

You can clearly see the components of the cycle. The dormant phase was not actually dormant. Instead it was one of a series of out of awareness feeling states. The principal driver of Ben's addictive cycle was shame. Ben had a physical abnormality. While it was invisible in everyday life, it was visible to him; his chest was slightly concave. He endured years of teasing in the changing rooms of his secondary school. This physical defect contributed to a sense of deficiency that ran through and dominated his life. The precursor state to Ben's acting out was a pervading and overwhelming sense of shame, of being defective. The seemingly unimportant decision was to go to the newsagent to buy the paper. The trigger was the top shelf. The rest of the cycle has been described. It was endlessly repetitive and highly ritualised. Ben's life was a life lived in shame, with periods of escape into sexual behaviour. These periods of escape simply kept the cycle going because each period of escape confirmed to Ben that his life was shameful.

Once Ben had become aware of the cycle, it could be stopped. Do not go out for a paper. Do not let the arousal chemistry build up so that the acting out becomes inevitable. Do something else at lunch time: go for a run, go to the gym or take a brisk walk. Ring up someone in recovery every day at lunchtime. After a time of alternative behaviour, the addictive pattern will fade. What is more, self-esteem will increase and shame will diminish. Ben needed good quality cognitive behavioural therapy to change the feelings of low self-worth and the exercises provided by CBT to challenge his lifelong belief of 'I am not enough'.

Exercise: cycle of addiction

I would like you prepare your own personal cycle of addiction. Take a recent or memorable time that you acted out. Consider your mood state before acting out. Consider the seemingly unimportant decisions and the triggers and then fill in the cycle to the point of inevitability. Add the actual acting out and then describe the feelings afterwards. You should also put in the things that make up reconstitution. Not everyone has all the components of Ben's cycle to the same degree. Sometimes the movement from feeling states to acting out can take place in seconds. This is especially true for those who act out on the internet. Sometimes the build-up part of the cycle can take forever. This is true for some men who act out when travelling on business. They can start, weeks in advance, looking for a sex worker. Some men do not have an especially strong sense of remorse after acting out. However, the general features of the cycle still hold.

It might be helpful to do several examples of sexual acting out. You will probably find that the cycles are much the same.

Describe the acting out experience:

_____

_____

_____

_____

_____

What were the precursors?

_____

_____

_____

_____

_____

What were the seemingly unimportant decisions?

_____

_____

_____

_____

_____

What were the triggers?

_____

_____

_____

_____

_____

What did you notice during the build-up phase?

_____

_____

_____

_____

_____

What happened at the point of inevitability?

_____

_____

_____

_____

_____

What were your thoughts, feelings and behaviours during the sexual acting out phase?

_____

_____

_____

_____

_____

After-effects: what were the feelings after acting out?

_____

_____

_____

_____

_____

What did you notice about your thoughts, feelings and behaviours during the reconstitution phase?

_____

_____

_____

_____

_____

Recap of tasks for week 6

* Look at the Lecture on the Cycle of Addiction on YouTube (www. youtube.com/results?search_query=cycle+of+addiction+birchard).
* Personalise the Cycle.
* Continue to keep the urge diary.
* Read Pillar 6 three times a day.

Pillar for week 6

I realise that my acting out runs in cycles. I understand that the process involves difficult or intolerable feeling states. I recognise that I use sexual behaviour to escape these negative feelings. I am not going to keep on doing that. I am beginning to understand my addictive sexual behaviour and I am starting to understand the sequence of events that take me into sexual acting out. I can learn and, though learning, I can change. I commit myself to this ongoing programme of change. I can be the person I want to be. I can make my outer self and my inner self match. I can, with effort and commitment, make the necessary changes. That is my resolve.

This week's learning summary:

_____

_____

_____

_____

_____

_____

_____

_____

_____

Exiting the cycle

Now that you have an understanding of your own cycle of addiction, it is important to begin to think about how you can break it. There are numerous points at which you can interrupt the cycle in order to ensure that you do not repeat your addictive behaviours. In general, the earlier you interrupt the cycle, the better. Once the arousal chemistry starts to build, it shuts down your ability to think about the consequences of the actions and it therefore becomes harder to find a way out of the inevitable. For this reason, it is important to take early avoiding actions so that you are not overwhelmed by the arousal chemistry. The more it builds up, the more difficult it is to break free. This chapter looks at some of the key ways in which you can break your addiction cycle.

The first line of defence against sexual acting out is to recognise when you are in a precursor state, such as loneliness, anxiety, depression, low mood, boredom or feeling alienated from your partner. Once you have noticed the feeling state that usually precedes sexual acting out, you can consider and implement a different strategy. If you feel bored, do something that will be demanding. Go for a run, play a game of squash, organise a game of chess or get in the car and drive to a new place. The best remedy for anxiety that I know is to run. If you do not want to run, try meditation or breathing exercises instead. If you are lonely, go to a meeting, go to church, ring an old friend, talk to a neighbour or meet a friend for coffee. You have to do something different in order to stop the cycle from continuing.

Recovery groups often provide a good way of managing unbearable feeling states. In every group that we run, we have two or three men who act out sexually on loneliness. This is not a passing sense of loneliness but something deeper and far-reaching. It is a deep inner sense of being alone, and the need for company is not always met in the couple relationship or even in a crowd of people. As I have said elsewhere, addiction is often set up and driven by disconnectedness. Darren was one of the men in treatment who acted out on loneliness. For him, there was a semblance of connectedness in the sexual act, but it only resembled connectedness. He used the physical components of one-night stands and encounters with sex workers to achieve something that looked like connectedness, but was actually counterfeit. The group process in our treatment programme creates an environment where men are no longer alone. They are asked to be honest with each other and they learn that intimacy is built up in honest communication and not in prevarication. Darren had never known male bonding and this was his first experience of genuine comradeship. This experience alone was enough to intervene in his addictive use of sex workers and one-night stands.

So, the best exit point from the sex addiction cycle is to recognise the prior feeling state and try to alter it without resorting to sexual behaviour. Remember that the earlier that you exit the cycle, the safer you will be. The immediate reward of sexual pleasure is so great that it eclipses any thought of the aftermath. The same thing happens with alcohol. Once you have had a couple of glasses of wine your thinking gets distorted and you have a couple more. Any thoughts about the hangover the next morning are forgotten. It is only the next morning when you wake up with a terrible headache and upset stomach that you think to yourself, 'I should not have done that, it was the last time, I will never do that again'. Whether we are talking about drinking to excess or acting out sexually, the same thing applies. The power of the immediate reward is so great that it obscures or obliterates the reality of the aftermath. You need to exit before the arousal chemistry can take you to the point of no return.

Once you know and learn more about your cycle of addiction, you will begin to notice the seemingly unimportant decisions that precede your sexual acting out and then you will have the opportunity to change them. For example, many men in treatment have come to realise that something as simple as flirting takes them towards acting out sexually. Giving compliments about looks can be changed to giving compliments about non-arousing features, which can be just as gracious but do not lead into the possibility of a sexual encounter. You can notice and point out her sense of humour, her kindness or her commitment to her husband. These statements are complimentary but they do not give off signals that can lead to sexual misadventure. Learning about the cycle of addiction will help you learn to notice and then to avoid these seemingly unimportant decisions. Remember that these decisions take you into triggers, and triggers take you into addictive sexual behaviour.

There may be both people and places that you will need to avoid because they act as triggers to sexual acting out. Much the same is true with alcohol. If you want to leave it behind, you will probably have to change your friends. You cannot go to restaurants and public houses where you drank. I gave up alcohol last year and I find that I have to avoid certain restaurants where I used to drink. Just being there acts as a trigger.

Very often you have to put in place a new set of alternative behaviours that take you out of the old patterns of behaviour and avoid the triggers to sexual acting out. We had one patient who used to drive up to London on the M4 motorway. He had done this many times before and turned off to go to a sex club. He had to come to London by another route because the old route triggered his addictive processes. He had to change his routine to avoid encountering situations and places that took him into sexual acting out.

The addiction cycle is particularly problematic for those of you who are addicted to internet pornography, because the time factors are so quick that there is almost no time for reflection, and the transition from normal discomfort to sexual oblivion is virtually instantaneous. If you are addicted to internet pornography, it is important to have a blocker on your system. Of course, you can get around the blocker but there is a time delay, which creates an opportunity to think again. You will be able to decide whether you really need to do this, in the knowledge that it will only make you unhappy tomorrow.

Let's look at an example of a patient who successfully broke his cycle of internet pornography addiction. Rupert lived life in a state of permanent low mood or semi-depression. His mindset was that his glass was always half empty. He had a tendency to be gloomy and his life was lived largely without joy. He had a job that he did not enjoy, he saw his family as a burden, he took no exercise and had no satisfying outside activities. He would sell insurance and then come home and watch television until his wife went to bed. Then the excitement would start when he could open his laptop and watch pornography. He always intended to watch porn for an hour and then go to bed, but he would get caught up in the vortex of porn and send pictures of himself to women, in the hope that he would receive pictures back from them. Eventually, at about 2am, he would shut down the computer and go to bed. He had to get up at 6am to go to work. After four hours' sleep, his work the next day suffered and he said 'never again' until he would go home the next night and the pattern would be repeated. He was in the thrall of internet porn. His low mood was relieved and replaced with the exhilaration of sexual excitement, but this was a temporary escape from an otherwise tedious life.

Rupert had to learn a new way of living. Over time, he learned to take joy in small things. He put blockers on his computer and began to go to bed with his wife. He decided to go to evening classes and learn a new skill so that he could change his employment. He even took up bridge. Rupert learned to fill his life with meaningful activity. This new way of living gave him great satisfaction and a sense of achievement and control over his life and, in due course, the internet pornography receded into the past. To his wife's surprise, sexual energy also returned to the marriage bed. Everyone was happier.

Let us look at a couple of examples of men who have been in treatment at our clinic and who managed to put in place successful exit strategies and break their cycles of sexual addiction. First, there is Nick. He joined our group treatment programme and came though it with flying colours. Nick was a young man of just 23. He was good looking in a rugged sort of way and something of a 'lad'. He was irrepressibly earnest and remarkably honest in reporting the ups and downs of sexual recovery to the group. He was a committed Christian and worked for a large Evangelical Church in central London. He had become increasingly aware that his outer self did not match his inner self. While he worked with the Church youth group, he was addicted to internet pornography and this morphed into the regular use of sex workers. There were also casual sexual encounters with various women from the Church. Nick understood the cycle of addiction, and he realised that the first step to recovery was for him to get rid of his smart-phone. The smartphone allowed him to access internet pornography and to cruise escort sites. This would lead to paying for sex. Getting rid of the smartphone was therefore his first priority in his strategy of change. This was followed by other wholesale changes. He blocked internet sites on his computer and took to using his laptop in the communal room of his shared flat. Eventually he decided to quit his work for the Church. The Church work had set up an impossible conflict between who he was and what he was meant to represent. He eventually moved house and then moved cities. He now commutes into our treatment programme. Nick was prepared to go to any length. For Nick, higher order values triumphed over sexual addiction. He has not completely recovered but he has moved to a place where he is not dominated by his sexuality. For Nick, sexuality has become part of life and, with humility, he has accepted the reality of the difference between who he is and who he strives to be. His goal is one relationship with one woman lived in fidelity. He was prepared to go to any length to achieve this.

Some individuals seem to have a lower boredom threshold than others. Some of us can be joyfully excited pruning the roses and others have to do extreme activities like sky diving or bungee jumping to make life interesting and exciting. These patients tend to arrive at my clinic on motorcycles.

Whenever I hear a patient pull up on a motorcycle a voice inside of me asks the question 'Is this man boredom prone?' Gerrard arrived on a super-sized motorcycle and used to ride off to Brussels going down the motorway at 100mph. He was always taking action-filled holidays. He worked as a trader in the City and his daily life was full of anticipatory excitement. His sexual addiction was always in the extreme, usually combined with alcohol and cocaine. He had sex with over 150 women in the past six months. I wonder how he found the time. He seemed to be addicted to adrenalin and without these vast levels of excitement, he found life tedious and dull. Pruning the roses was not enough for him. He acted out sexually on boredom proneness. He began to understand this and eventually was able to replace sexual adventure with other stimulating activities. These new activities never gave him the intensity of the high he got from cocaine and women but they gave him, overall, a much better quality of life.

In a Twelve Step programme like Sex Addicts Anonymous, there is a saying that you 'have to be willing to go to any length' to overcome your addiction. Start to have a think about the lengths that you are prepared to go to personally.

We are coming to the end of this section. You will hopefully now have a good idea of your cycle of addiction, the precursors, the seemingly unimportant decisions, the triggers and the aftermath. You are beginning to consider exit strategies and changes of behaviour that will keep you free of unwanted patterns of sexual behaviour. A last word to the wise: get rid of your stash. By this I mean, delete all numbers of previous sexual contacts, block their incoming calls and delete all inappropriate web addresses. Even change your mobile number. I know this is a hassle but you have to be willing to go to any length. Getting rid of the stash is difficult and painful. There is always a feeling of loss. It is almost a grieving process because you are saying goodbye to an old friend. Sexual acting out has given you a lot of pleasure, so simply accept that doing this will cause you considerable grief. That will soon be replaced by the realisation that you have done the right thing and that the double life is coming to an end.

Exercise: exit strategies

I would now like you to examine the cycle that you produced in the previous chapter and consider potential exit points. Remember that the best exit point is to recognise the prior feeling state and to try to alter it without resorting to sexual behaviour. The earlier you exit the cycle, the safer you will be. Take a look at each stage of the cycle (precursors, seemingly unimportant decisions, triggers, build-up, point of inevitability and acting out) and consider whether there are ways in which you could have exited it.

Precursors: exit strategy

_____

_____

_____

_____

_____

Seemingly unimportant decisions: exit strategy

_____

_____

_____

_____

_____

Triggers: exit strategy

_____

_____

_____

_____

_____

Build-up: exit strategy

_____

_____

_____

_____

_____

Point of inevitability: exit strategy

_____

_____

_____

_____

_____

Acting out: exit strategy

_____

_____

_____

_____

_____

Recap of tasks for week 7

*   Write out your exit strategies.
*   Continue to keep the urge diary.
*   Recite Pillar 7 three times a day.

Pillar for week 7

I am beginning to realise that my addictive sexual behaviour is based on a repeating pattern of behaviour that I have never really understood. As I try to understand it, I will try to leave it behind. I commit myself to a new way of living. This new way of living involves considerable sacrifice but it brings hope for the future. I have begun to understand the feeling states that lead me into sexual addiction, the seemingly unimportant decisions, the cues and triggers that lead me into the inevitable but unwanted sexual behaviour. But I have decided to change and with the help of this programme I will commit to making this change. I want to turn the 'after-effects of shame' into good feelings of success. I commit myself to this and to a life in recovery.

This week's learning summary:

_____

_____

_____

_____

_____

_____

_____

_____

_____

_____

Cognitive distortions

As we learned in Chapter 2, the way in which we interpret our experiences, as well as our own and other people's behaviour, is determined by our thinking. When we are caught up in a cycle of addiction, it is likely that there are some errors in our thinking. These often appear as irrational excuses offered for our sexual behaviour in a moment of panic. This section examines the most common thinking errors that generally accompany inappropriate sexual activity. Psychologists normally refer to these errors as 'cognitive distortions'. I personally call them 'cognitive deceptions', because they emerge from our inner world and do not necessarily reflect reality. We will see how they emerge from feelings of shame and are designed to protect us from the true burden of the behaviour, through a denial of responsibility. We will also see how these thinking errors arise from our core beliefs about ourselves.

When we are confronted with the evidence that we have acted out sexually, it is likely that we will begin to develop feelings of shame. As I wrote in Part I of this book, shame is the excruciating feeling of helpless condemnation. There are a number of common ways in which we try to handle the discomfort of shame. They all involve twisting our thinking so that we do not have to experience the unbearable sensation of shame. The most common ways in which we do this are through denial, rationalisation, justification, minimisation, excuses and blame. We shall examine each of these briefly in turn.

Denial involves saying that the sexual acting out just did not happen. Sometimes you really may believe this, but at other times you may use this to protect yourself from blame.

Rationalisation involves admitting that the sexual acting out happened, but convincing yourself that you will never do it again. Think of all the times you might have said that to yourself as you came away from the flat of a sex worker or out of a public lavatory. It is quite easy to believe that it really will not happen again until you take a good look at your cycle of addiction. Awareness of the cycle will highlight how long it has been going on. If you examine the evidence over the years of acting out, you will probably see that you have said this numerous times and, without proper intervention, you will continue deceiving yourself and repeating the behaviour.

Justification means admitting that, although the sexual acting might have happened, you definitely didn't intend to do it. An example of this would be telling yourself that you must have been stressed and she just took it the wrong way. Perhaps you justify the behaviour by telling yourself that your wife will not have sex with you and you are horny. This is to deny responsibility and to try to present the situation in the best possible light. It is a face-saving routine.

Minimisation involves admitting to the sexual acting but playing down the consequences. For example, you might tell yourself that, although you had sex with a girl, no harm was really done and she will forget all about it in a few weeks. You may admit to yourself that she was rather young, but you cannot imagine there will be any lasting damage. The research on inappropriate sexual contact tells us differently. People can be badly damaged by such contact and, in the long term, it can cause them to avoid intimacy and can bring about other psychosexual problems.

You may use excuses as a way to guard against the consequences of your sexual acting out. For example, you may admit to yourself that you did have sex with a boy, but you say that you were drunk and did not know what you were doing. You say that you really will have to stop drinking. However, you do not take responsibility for the fact that you chose to get drunk, despite knowing that alcohol disinhibits and allows people to do all sorts of things that they would not consider when sober.

If you use blame to deflect from the consequences of your sexual acting out, you will say that it was not your fault. Perhaps you will say that the woman was leading you on. After all, she should not go around in a skirt that was so short that you could just about see everything. Women often dress to attract, but there is a difference between being attracted, and even chatting her up, and putting your hand up her skirt.

All of the above distortions are designed to protect the self from the shame involved in the admission of the sexual act. They might be thinking errors but they are also natural responses to the significant threat of shame. These responses are more common with people whose sexual patterns take them into offending behaviours; nevertheless, I am sure that most of you will have had thoughts like this.

All of these strategies are about the denial of responsibility. They emerge from an unwillingness to accept that you have caused offence, as this would mean facing your shame. The best thing to do is to acknowledge that you have caused hurt, apologise and, with responsibility and humility, handle the consequences.

A useful model for understanding our responses to shame is the shame compass. It illustrates the four main ways in which different people manage shame.

At the top of the compass is the tendency to hide. Many of us respond to shame by hiding from others or ourselves. The body language of shame is the covered mouth and the hidden face. All of the usual mechanisms for dealing with shame are about hiding, for example, telling ourselves 'it was not me', 'it did no harm', 'I was drunk' or 'she should not have been wearing that short skirt'. As we have seen, all of these are excuses that seek to avoid the experience of shame. At the bottom of the compass is escape. This means that we escape from the feelings of shame by drinking alcohol or disappearing into sexually compulsive behaviour. To the right of the compass is 'Blame Another' and to the left, 'Blame Self'. A simple example of both of these is name calling. This applies to the use of negative terms addressed to the self or about the other.

Each of us will make use of different thinking errors, or cognitive distortions, to defend against the shame attached to sexual acting out. It is my view that each cognitive distortion comes out of our negative core beliefs. Remember that our core beliefs shape the way in which we see ourselves, others and the world around us. They are deep-rooted, usually formed in early childhood as a result of the way in which we experienced our relationships with our parents or primary caregivers. They tend to be hidden to us, but they will determine the type of thinking errors we use. Common

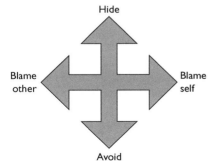

Figure 2.8.1 Compass of shame.
Source: Nathanson 1992: 312.

core beliefs are 'I'm not good enough', 'I'm unlovable', 'I'm a failure', 'I'm worthless' and 'I don't deserve anything good'.

We can explore the relationship between thinking errors and core beliefs in greater depth by using a model of cognitive distortions produced by Sanders and Wills (2005). I will take their comprehensive list of cognitive distortions, expand upon them and comment on them in reference to the core belief. The most common thinking errors are the following:

Black and White Thinking: this means seeing things in black and white and ignoring the reality that, in fact, things are always in shades of grey. Black and white thinkers are often persecutors of themselves or of others. You could be a black/white thinker yourself and either blame your wife entirely for your sexual acting out or you could bury yourself in shame and overwhelming blame of yourself for your behaviour. Neither are appropriate. We are all a combination of strengths and weaknesses and that is the reality of the human condition. You may be married to a black/white thinker. In my experience, men who have been discovered to have acted out sexually and are married to black/white thinkers tend to live with persecution for many years. These people go to polarised positions, seeing things as either completely bad or completely good. In reality, people are neither completely good nor completely bad. This is an unforgiving mindset. Alternatively, the partner who is a black/white thinker can simply blame herself for all her troubles and sink into a mighty depression. These extreme thinkers are hard to live with.

Mind Reading: mind reading is to make assumptions about the opinions and views of others based not on the facts, but on your own core belief. For example, you receive an email which you interpret as hostile. In fact this is your interpretation based on your inner view of yourself. You might react to the email by thinking 'He is the most awful person for sending me this'. Or alternatively you might think, 'Oh dear, I must have done something terribly wrong'. Both of these responses emerge from your inner belief about yourself and others. It is just an internal voice which is not based on evidence. It is the tendency to blame another or blame oneself.

Gazing into the Crystal Ball: this cognitive distortion involves always predicting negative outcomes in the future. This is partly attached to having experienced a large number of negative reactions and consequences in the past. However, when you look at the evidence, some things turn out badly and some things turn out well. This would be a much more realistic position to hold, rather than believing that everything is going to turn out badly. An expectation of negative outcomes is based on an all-pervasive fear. It might be low-grade but it is an expectation that all will not be well. It is normally connected to the fact that our expectations coincide with our core belief. The core belief is generally 'I am bad, therefore nothing will ever work out for me again'.

Mental Filter: this cognitive distortion involves the tendency to over-focus on the negative or to interpret events in the negative without evidence. Out of a whole plethora of events, circumstances, people and places, the person with a mental filter will only focus on the things that are negative, as these reinforce his core belief, which might be something like 'the world is a hostile place, other people are hostile' or 'I am not worthy of respect'. This means that you will ignore the neutral and the positive and notice only that which accords with or derives from the negative core belief. For example, imagine that you go shopping in ten shops. You get perfectly acceptable service in the first nine shops but in the tenth shop, the sales assistant is rude to you. If you have a mental filter, you will forget about the other nine and focus on the tenth. Your mind filters out the positive and leaves you stranded on the negative. You then ruminate on the tenth, telling yourself something like, 'It was not fair, he was so rude'. This chimes with your core belief, which is likely to be 'I am not worthy of respect'. If you did not hold your core belief about yourself, you could just have easily thought 'Poor dear, she is having a bad day. Her rudeness is not at all about me.'

Minimising the Positive: in this type of cognitive distortion, you minimise your own achievements and disregard them as meaningless. You dismiss some quality or skill that you have as not important, having no weight. This is generally related to the core belief that 'I am not good'. This core belief speaks very loudly and sometimes it makes it impossible to hear or see the good about yourself. For example, perhaps you go fly fishing. You might not consider that an important skill but not everyone can do it and many of us do not have the patience to learn. I know this because I have gone fly fishing and I learned that it involves patience and physical dexterity, as well as good hand–eye co-ordination. I could not do it and in one week I caught absolutely nothing. If I were really interested I could, with repetition and frequency, become a fly fisher. There are a lot of positive qualities that we underrate: fatherhood, providing for the family, playing squash, political activism, helping the children with their homework, keeping fit and building up the family finances. None of these are to be downgraded and none are without merit. After all, we are a lot more than our sexuality.

Magnification: with this thinking error you over-dramatise the importance of small events and interpret them to mean something disastrous about yourself. For example, you might tell yourself, 'I cannot remember where I put my phone, I must have early onset Alzheimer's'. Partly this is connected to an expectation of disaster and perhaps to a belief that you are getting what you deserve. Like the previous cognitive distortion, magnification of negative events grows out of the core belief that we are bad. It is the same as minimisation except it is an interpretation projected onto the future. You probably do this in a negative way. Few of us wake up in the morning feeling fine and think that we are experiencing the advantage of having an alcohol-free evening, and then celebrate an alcohol-free future. We wake up with a hangover and feel depressed, telling ourselves that life is futile. In other words, magnification is the tendency to use the small events as predictors of appalling future consequences. In reality, the future will be what it will be and we have no control over unexpected illness, accident or the timing of our eventual mortality.

Emotional Reasoning: emotional reasoning is very easy to understand. It simply means that you interpret a feeling as if it were a fact. You feel bad, therefore you are bad. You feel guilty, therefore you are guilty. This can be hard to conquer as your feeling state is powerful and can direct your thoughts. I had my computer stolen from my office. There was no evidence that I had done anything wrong, but my core belief that 'I am a fuck-up' is so strong that the feelings of shame overpowered my cognitive capacity to weigh up the evidence. However, I did know that my core belief had been triggered and there was no evidence that I had done anything irresponsible. Still the feeling lingered on. It took four days for it to clear. I knew that it was a deception and that I was responding to the legacy of childhood messaging and not to the reality of the present day situation. At least I knew that I was having a shame attack and that the real-life evidence did not support the feeling state.

Unrealistic Expectations: unrealistic expectations are usually made up of many 'shoulds' and 'musts'. These unrealistic expectations usually come from a childhood which values us for our capacity to perform. You should have achieved an 'A' in biology but only got a 'B' and therefore you are a failure. I know I should give to the poor but there are eight beggars between the office and the tube station. To give to them all everyday would seem an unrealistic expectation laid down in my previous training. I can only give to some and I have decided to give to two and not to beat myself up about the other six. Unrealistic expectation is a way of keeping the core belief that you are not good enough in place by exaggerating the rating criteria.

Name Calling: whenever we call ourselves or others names, we are contributing to a perpetuation of the core belief, be it theirs or ours. Let us take the example of 'Lola'. If Lola forgot her keys or her handbag, she used to say to herself 'I am such an idiot'. We all forget things. I have frequently left my keys at home, my wallet in the bedroom or my mobile phone on the table in the café. None of these things actually tell me that I am an idiot. They tell me that there is a lot on my mind, that I am too busy or just distracted. Lola was also not an idiot. She had a first-class degree from Cambridge and was working in finance. It was simply her inner voice, or inner persecutor, talking to her. It was her shame speaking to her and it had no relationship to the reality of her ability or her capacity to manage life. In this case, it was her core belief that she was 'not good enough' which led her to think that she was a complete idiot. There was no evidence at all to support this ridiculous idea, but her repeated self-talk held it in place and her thinking errors reinforced her core belief about herself.

Self-blame: a lot of people blame themselves even when they are not responsible for the action. This is the core belief talking to us. I had a patient who apologised to me when my phone rang. I had forgotten to turn it off when he came into the consulting room. He apologised to me, even though it was nothing to do with him. It was my fault. His core belief that he was inadequate and less than others was not only evidenced in the apology but held in place by this constant self-criticism. My own core belief was so powerful and so automatic that I once apologised to a step I had tripped over. That is clearly ridiculous. We are all a mixture of the good and the not so good. That is a fact of life. Self-blame is the tendency to ignore this and to only notice the negative in one's self and to magnify this until it ends up out of all proportion to the total picture. Sexual issues are power-packed with the potential for this.

Catastrophising: this is the simple tendency to anticipate the worst possible outcome to any situation. This too is related to the core belief that you are bad and therefore the outcome is bound to be bad. The reality is that some things turn out bad and some turn out well. If you were to make a chart of all the times that you expected the worst possible outcome and found that it did not happen and add this to the overall collection of evidence, you would probably be surprised that in many, if not most cases, the catastrophe never actually occurred.

So, in conclusion, our thinking errors or cognitive distortions emerge from our core beliefs. They are anchored in the core belief and they function to sustain the core belief. They are all interpretations or projections of the shame compass. Mind reading is an interpretation of the state of the other based upon your own core belief. Gazing into the crystal ball is a propensity to see the future in the terms of your core belief. The same is true of the mental filter, except that it is more about now than the future. Minimising and magnification both disregard the reality of the evidence. Assuming that what you feel is true similarly disregards the evidence or, at least, it disregards the total picture. Name calling helps to consciously or unconsciously keep you down. Self-blame is different from taking responsibility. It is a character assassination by you of your own character. Predicting the worst possible outcome is a spin-off of the core belief that 'I am a bad person and bad things are going to happen to me'. All of these thinking errors are projections, interpretations or expectations based on your core belief.

Exercise: cognitive distortions

I would like you to consider the list of the most common cognitive distortions and work out which ones are especially relevant in your thinking and speaking processes. Write real-life examples.

Black and White Thinking

_____

_____

_____

_____

_____

Mind Reading

_____

_____

_____

_____

_____

Gazing into the Crystal Ball

_____

_____

_____

_____

_____

Mental Filter

_____

_____

_____

_____

_____

Minimising the Positive

_____

_____

_____

_____

_____

Magnification

_____

_____

_____

_____

_____

Emotional Reasoning

_____

_____

_____

_____

_____

Unrealistic Expectations

_____

_____

_____

_____

_____

Name Calling

_____

_____

_____

_____

_____

Self-blame

_____

_____

_____

_____

_____

Catastrophising

_____

_____

_____

_____

_____

Recap of tasks for week 8

- Complete the exercises on cognitive distortions.
- Continue to keep the urge diary.
- Recite Pillar 8 three times a day.

Pillar for week 8

I understand that my feelings follow my thoughts and also that my feelings can affect my thoughts. I will try in the future to look at the evidence that surrounds my behaviour and take a more balanced perspective. I might have done some 'not so good things' but these do not totally cancel out my character as an upright person. There is more to my life than my sexual behaviour. In fact, I realise that these negative thinking patterns and the feelings associated with them can lead me back into addictive processes. I understand that my sexual addiction was a way of changing my feeling states, and by changing my thinking patterns, I can help prevent myself from falling again into addictive compulsive sexual behaviour. I am doing better. I am healing from the wounds of the past and learning new ways to take care of myself. I will do this, not just for me, but also for those I love.

This week's learning summary:

_____

_____

_____

_____

_____

_____

_____

_____

_____

_____

Personal history

We tend to imagine that we are responsible for the fact that we have our sexual patterns. Our core belief probably holds this in place and persuades us that this is the case. You might say that this is another cognitive distortion. The reality is that no one is responsible for having a pattern of desire, even if it is quirky. It was set up in the family of origin and emerges from our distinctive childhood experiences. This is not to say that you are not responsible about how you manage it or how you come to terms with it; it does not absolve you from living with it in a responsible and properly controlled manner. Nobody would actually choose a pattern of sexual behaviour that would cause a multitude of problems, whether it is acting out in saunas, having sex in public venues, using the services of sex workers or endless nights looking at internet pornography. You might do any one of these, or all of them, but you did not ask for the behaviour or the desire to do it. It was set up and you have inherited it as a legacy of your developmental history. However, human beings are more than their developmental history and have a responsibility to act according to the higher order values of responsibility, respect, honesty and integrity.

In working with sex addicts, almost the first thing that I do is to take a history. This is a three-hour process. The first half of the session is given to the general history and the second half to the sexual and relationship history. I then go away and analyse the history and prepare a report. I can always determine the causation and the key components that have created the addictive process. However, I have found that the most important information is in the general history, rather than in the sexual history. This leads me to the conclusion that the sexual and relationship history is an outworking of the general history.

In the general history, I am particularly interested in the birth story and any trauma that might precede it. I look for interruptions in the bonding between mother and child. I am interested in any complications at the time

of the birth, whether the child was breastfed and whether there were prolonged separations in early infancy. I am interested in the patterns of discipline used in the family. Repetitive harsh treatment can amount to child
abuse. One patient was slapped in the face weekly from the age of 4 to 16.
To be hit in the face is especially damaging because the face represents the
self. Some patients were locked in their rooms as children or, in the old
days, in the coal cellar. Even when there were no childhood circumstances
of physical punishment, there might have been endless criticism and
admonition. Sometimes abusive parental behaviour can combine physical
punishment and spiritual abuse. One man was taken outside, beaten and
made to recite the 'Hail Mary' during the beating. I am also interested in
the child's exposure to parental conflict or abusive attacks upon siblings. It
is unsettling, to say the least, if your parents are involved in continuous
conflict or your brother or sister is mistreated in your presence. I ask
euphemistically about 'bathroom' habits because prolonged bedwetting
can be a sign of child–family disruption. The same is true for inter-
domestic theft, where the child repeatedly steals from the parent. I need to
know the medical history of the man as a child. Prolonged separations or
traumatic times spent in hospital disrupt and impair the child and hence the
adult's sense of self. I always ask directly about sexual and physical abuse,
although I rarely come across it in practice.

I had one patient with a chronic disease, who had had multiple opera-
tions in childhood. These left him with a fear of the future. He developed
an overwhelming interest in internet pornography as a learned escape from
this fear and from his sense of being defective, which had been set up in
his childhood circumstances. I noted that the invasive procedures he under-
went were at their worst between the ages of eight and nine, which is a
crucial period for the development of the sexual template.

There are other crucial elements to the life story that have come to
strike me as important. I always ask patients about their experience of
school. I look out for words like 'shy', 'outsider' or 'did not fit in'. These
kinds of phrases suggest that any experience of early shame had begun to
manifest itself directly with the development of self-consciousness. I also
ask about bullying. Bullying is an assault upon the self and can leave
lasting scars.

The single largest and most important factor in the development of the
sexually compulsive man is the characteristics of the parents. I usually ask
patients to give me five or six words, phrases or sentences that would
describe each parent. I include the stepparent, where appropriate. In this
list, I look for connecting words that would suggest good attachment to the
parent, but I am aware that in most cases, sexually compulsive men are

inheritors of unreliable, narcissistic or inadequate parenting. This is not the parents' 'fault' because, in my experience, parents are doing the best job they know how, but have inherited a set of limitations from their own parents.

I will give you an example from my clinical work to describe this process. I asked a patient, 'What was your mother like when you were a child? Can you give me five or six words or sentences that would describe her? If I were looking through the window, what kind of woman would I see?' The answers were: 'strict', 'unhappy', 'struggling with finances' and 'bullied my father'. I asked him the same questions about his dad. The answers were 'downtrodden', 'overruled', 'unfaithful' and 'uneducated'.

There are a number of things suggested in these descriptions. The first thing to note is that these were the only things that were said. There were no connecting words used to describe the parents' relationship with the child, except the word 'strict' which is used of the mother. His mother, in fact, hit him about once a week when he was between the ages of six and ten. His father came and went from the relationship with his mother. He never saw a functional relationship and was never able to internalise the procedures or the structure of fulfilling and harmonious relationships. He once said to me that he never knew what to expect when he came home. This might well have set up an avoidance of the uncertain and a preference for routine and the expected. He was addicted to online pornography.

You will find the reasons for your present circumstances by answering all of these questions about your childhood. It is true that the child is the father of the man. Sexual addiction and all addictions are set up in disconnectedness and the imposition on the child of a sense of not measuring up, of being wrong or somehow being a disappointment to the mother or father. All addiction forms itself in this sense of personal deficiency; for sex addicts, sexual behaviour is the mode of escape from these difficult feelings.

I have permission from one of my patients – Liam – to share his story, to demonstrate the connections between addictive behaviour and the creation of that behaviour in early life. Most of us will not have experienced anything as drastic as Liam but I have chosen this story because it illustrates the traumas of childhood and the ensuing chaos that enveloped him. Liam is in recovery and has done well through our treatment programme and the other groups that he attends.

Liam is a 40-year-old, Irish, heterosexual male. He is the middle of three adopted children and has an older sister and a younger one. He went to a same-sex secondary school and was a boarder from age 13 to 17. He is currently not in a relationship. Although he did not go to university, he has done well in business and made a great deal of money. He is a recovering alcoholic and has been in Alcoholics Anonymous for the past six years. He goes to meetings about five times a week. He has made a good recovery. He uses the gym about five times a week and is physically fit and slim. He tends to be a perfectionist and enjoys things being neat, clean and tidy. He is an intelligent and capable man with great insight and a rich spirituality. He has a delightful and understated sense of humour. His interests are music and opera, especially Wagner.

Liam was adopted when he was a year old. His birth mother was 15 and from a poor Irish farming community. Her father threw her out when he learned that she was pregnant and she was 'sent to the nuns'. She nursed him for about two weeks after birth. Presumably, he was bottle-fed after that time. His mother would have been described as a 'fallen woman' and a 'young slut'. His birth father ran away. It is unlikely that his mother had any sex education and she would have been ignorant about contraception. He was then adopted by a dangerous and violent woman who was monstrous towards him and his adopted sisters. Although it was the perfect family on the outside, this perfection concealed many secrets.

Liam told me, 'I was adopted for religion. We were told on a daily basis that we were adopted.' Liam said that he always felt out of place at school. He describes his adopting mother as domineering, frightening, vengeful, cold, mental and barbaric. There was nothing positive said about her. There were no good times. There were constant shouts and constant threats of being hit and beaten. His adoptive mother used to say, with great frequency, 'I will murder you, I will cut you in two, and I will make you black and blue'. Liam told me, 'It was malicious. I can still remember the ringing in my ears.' Everything had to be done fast. She fell out with everyone and did not attend her own mother's funeral.

One of Liam's early memories was his adopting mother teaching him how to read the time. He told me,

> She had a clock and if we got the wrong answer she would hit us across the face. We were threatened with being hit and we were hit all the time. We were hit everywhere with a wooden spoon: arms, legs, across the face. I still remember the rings on her fingers. It was all to do with her and not letting her down. I wanted her approval and I never got it.

The violence in the family was random and unpredictable but the threat of violence was constant. Liam told me, 'I was kicked and I don't want to remember it'. Later when he was older, his adoptive mother went to the school to ask the teachers to beat him more. He told me, 'I never understood love, mothers with their children'.

The eldest sister seemed to be the more normal of his two siblings, although she did say that she had been abused by their adopting father. The younger sister is described as a criminal and a fraudster. Liam said that his adopting father was gentle and kind but was dominated by the mother. He left the family home twice during the marriage. This man did nothing to protect the children from the adopting mother's onslaughts.

Something should be said about the role of religion in Liam's life. His memories of the Church are good memories. He describes it as 'a place of peace and safety'. He said that the clergy tried to help him. After secondary school, Liam tried his vocation at seminary and he said that he loved the Church. It is probable that the Church, through its kindness, saved Liam from even greater damage, by being the only reliable source of safety throughout a disturbed and violent childhood.

Liam had an asexual childhood and told me that 'sex did not exist'. There are no reported memories of childhood rehearsal play or sexual experimentation and no memories of early masturbation. The three memories that stand out are being terrified at age five or six, when he went into his adopting mother's bedroom and saw the sheets covered in blood. The second memory was seeing a 'beautiful and good' girl going to school. He told me that he used to get the train just to see her. Finally, at secondary school, there was a kind, young woman who rubbed liniment on his chest when he was sick. There was an absence of sex education. His adopting parents gave him a book about sex but the pages in the last part of the book were all stapled together. This patient had had no same-sex experience and he did not masturbate until he was 17. Three things came together at this time: alcohol, masturbation and the Marquise de Sade. These things have been the centrepiece of his sexuality ever since. He had his first blackout from alcohol when he was 17.

Liam developed a preference for spanking women. He only had sex under the influence of alcohol. The woman had to be innocent, slim and blonde. He told me that 'there has to be schoolgirl innocence about it. I am extraordinarily aroused by pure innocence'. This search for innocence has not taken him into the realms of the illegal but he is aroused by women in school clothes and school shoes. There seem to be two parts to his behaviour: pretending that he is punishing the girls and talking about punishing them. Sometimes he does cane them but the caning is perfunctory. It is more about 'telling her that she has been naughty and that I have to spank her'. The fantasy is about the threat of violence rather than the actual violence itself.

Additionally, Liam has a routine heterosexual script but it is less full of erotic charge. He also has a history of delayed ejaculation and of erectile failure on penetration. The delay in ejaculation characterises masturbation as well as coitus. Liam also spoke of self-harm ideation related to knives, scissors and razor blades. This is particularly strong after masturbation. He said, 'I want to cut my balls off'. In adult life Liam has had three prostate infections, during one of which blood ran from his penis. I asked Liam about his primary goals for therapy. He told me that they were to remove the delayed ejaculation, to remove his thoughts of self-harm and to remove the murderous rage he felt towards his adopting mother.

The first priority was to tackle the panic attacks that accompanied the self-harm ideation. This was of utmost urgency. We used normal cognitive behavioural processes to help him diminish his anxiety, including the use of the formulation to make the behaviour understandable. As the self-harm ideation came after masturbation, we made a list of affirmations to say before and after masturbation. He has found these affirmations helpful. Liam also joined our treatment programme for men who are sexually addicted. He had clearly also been addicted to alcohol and was, to some extent, addicted to exercise.

We can easily see how spanking women is a conversion of Liam's childhood abuse into an eroticised victory. In his sexual fantasy Liam is able to get his own back on the abusive mother figure. I note that the behaviour is more about the threat of violence that the actuality of violence and that the desired object is innocent and beautiful. This is a total contrast to the adopting mother and, at the same time, harks back to his experience of kindness from women. It would seem that the imagery in the self-harm thoughts come from the adopting mother, threatening to cut him in two and to murder him. It is also a result of the profound sexual shame that she inculcated in him. The delayed ejaculation is difficult to treat but we have begun to tackle some of its causes: sexual shame, the need to be in control, body shame, the need for tidiness and the absence of contaminants. The main goal of psychotherapy is to discover and describe the beliefs that lie behind these enactments. It is to lessen shame and create higher levels of self-acceptance. The main reason such beliefs and enactments are difficult to change is that they provide powerful erotic pleasure.

Exercise: preparing a written history

The construction of a narrative is useful, revealing and reparative. A narrative is a written statement that covers your entire life, with a particular focus on your sexual history. Spend some time in a quiet place and think about your childhood, adolescence and adult life. It might be best to do this exercise over several hours or several days. You will need to go back to the trauma egg for information.

You will need time to sit with pencil and paper and write out the events and circumstances of your childhood with a focus on the negative. The negative events impact upon our development more than the positive because they register on the threat centre in the brain. For example, I was once mugged and spent time in hospital. Nine years later I am still uncomfortable hearing footsteps behind me when walking to work. I have to stop and let the person behind me pass by. While I have no memory of the mugging, part of me does remember. Negative experiences are threats to the self and therefore they register either consciously or unconsciously.

Writing everything out creates a sense of unity to the story. You will be able to see how the past connects to the present. You will be able to see patterns as well as connections. This will give coherence to the story. It might be a time of genuine catharsis as well because, for some of you, the memories might be bitter or painful to consider. We are not doing this to blame anyone but just to try to understand how it all fits together and causes the compulsive sexual behaviour.

The narrative might need to start off before you were born. There might be a history of broken marriages that continue from generation to generation. Your mother might have experienced trauma while she was pregnant with you. You will need to get information about your birth story, especially about the possibilities of prolonged separation from your mother, incubators, complications with the birth and information about breastfeeding. Keep in mind that we are looking for early trauma and complicating factors, like your own childhood ill health. You will need to consider and write out the events referred to in the trauma egg. You will also need to reflect on your early proto- or quasi-sexual experiences. These are things that you recognise now, looking back, as having sexual content. Then you will need to write out your sexual history, which includes childhood sexual games, early exploration and incidents that one might define as unwanted or abusive.

You will then need to write out the history of your sexually compulsive behaviour. Consider when it first started. Some patients become aware that they discovered masturbation early as a process to soothe themselves from the events happening around them. Some cultures have prohibitions against masturbation, which make its practice more shame-filled than in cultures that are relaxed about this activity. See if you can prepare a timeline of your sexual history, plotting along a line the relationship between your compulsive sexual behaviour and other events in your environment. Start at the beginning and take it up to the present.

Once this has been done, you will have your story. Finish the story of your sexual life with hopes and plans for the future. Think about your personal goals and the goals you might have for your personal development, for your professional or working life and for those who you love and who love you.

Sometimes people do further history processes. For example, I had one patient who wrote a history around all the men he had known in his life, including his dad who died when he was 10 and his grandfather who was (unnoticed at the time) a powerful influence on him. He later did another history around all the women in his life and found that his constant search for women seem to derive from an unavailable mother.

Many people find it helpful to share their story with a trusted person. In Sex Addicts Anonymous, this might be your sponsor or a group member. In our treatment programme each person tells their story to the group and the group members then give that person feedback on what it was like to hear the story. If you are doing this on your own, you might consider telling your story to a highly trusted friend. If you are in therapy, you could do this with your therapist. You could also do it with your pastor or parish priest. The other person will not find it a chore to hear because you are speaking from the heart. There is great power in hearing the truth spoken and there is almost always great respect for the humility involved. If you decide to do this, do be careful who you choose to talk to; this person must be trusted or committed to obligations of confidentiality.

There are various ways of pursuing your history but its function is to contribute to the creation of a coherent narrative. If you know how you are constituted, then you have some chance of making useful changes. If you do not know how you are made up and what developmental patterns contributed to the formation of the self, then it is extremely difficult to change. So knowing your history contributes to the possibility that you can become unstuck. What we know does not govern us to the same extent as what we do not know.

Recap of tasks for week 9

- Write out your personal history.
- Continue to keep the urge diary.
- Recite Pillar 9 three times a day.

Pillar for week 9

I know that I have a unique history. Nobody else has had, or can ever have, exactly the same history. Even if I have brothers and sisters, each of us interacted differently with our parents and caregivers, and that means we each had a different history. In this pillar I am focusing on some of the problems in my history. These were not of my making. They might have involved neglect, abuse, repetitious incidents of shame and threats of abandonment or impossibly high standards. I am not sure what caused it, but it left a legacy of weakness and hurt. However, I refuse to be bound by the past. I refuse to let the past be my captor. I will be free. Today I commit to the search for freedom. I seek to be liberated from years of addictive compulsive sexual behaviour. If I work for it, I can know a new freedom and a new happiness. I will continue to do this.

This week's learning summary:

_____

_____

_____

_____

_____

_____

_____

_____

_____

_____

Relapse prevention

We are coming to the end of the 10-week recovery programme. Before moving on to this chapter on relapse prevention, review the work done so far. You might reread the preliminary readings in the opening part of this book. You might revisit some of the exercises. You could go back to the provisional sex plan and consider, in the light of what you now know, whether it should be changed. You could have another go at the trauma egg and the cycle of addiction or the section on exit strategies. Although this self-help recovery programme is described as a 10-week programme, you are in charge. You can take as much time as necessary to complete it. In due course, you can do it all over again. Approach it in whatever way works best for you.

We will now focus on how to prevent relapse back into your old sexually addictive behaviours. Your relapse prevention plan will be unique to you. It will need to reflect your own distinctive needs and your own specific patterns of behaviour. Although there are overlaps and many commonalities, no two relapse prevention plans are the same. The mood states associated with acting out differ from person to person and the triggers are tied to our particular history. The content of the sexual behaviour will differ from person to person. Some of you will have acting out behaviours which are troublesome but are not especially dangerous. For those of you who have behaviours that threaten the safety of others and that could incur criminal penalties, relapse prevention is crucial to your own wellbeing and to the wellbeing of others.

To review, begin by thinking about the emotional states that make you particularly vulnerable to compulsive sexual behaviour. Some people act out primarily on anxiety and stress. The anxiety can be caused by internal memories or by negative interpretations of the actions and comments of others. Anxiety is usually cognitively based on an overestimation of future dangers and an underestimation of one's personal strength and resilience.

This combination creates fear and anxiety. Other people act out on loneliness, based upon a deep-seated existential feeling of being alone. This sense of loneliness is a constant companion in a relationship and in a crowd. Shame is another profoundly distressing feeling state; as we have seen, shame is not the feeling that you have made a mistake, but rather that you are a mistake. These are distressing feelings. These feelings make us want to crawl away and never be seen. At its worst, it is about profound public humiliation. It might be the feeling you had when your wife found out that you used sex workers or spent hours on the computer looking at bondage. These, and other negative feeling states, cause us to act out. Sex is the escape response.

In addition to negative feeling states, certain drugs can also act as a gateway into compulsive sexual behaviour. Alcohol is the most common of these drugs. Alcohol disinhibits. Under the influence of alcohol, all thoughts of consequences and the morrow are forgotten. Those of you who drink alcohol will know immediately that after the second drink all thought of consequences disappears. The second drink tells you that a couple of more would be even better. This is the road to becoming a drunk.

I had a patient – let's call him Jason – who went to a strip bar and after a couple of drinks, bought a couple of bottles of champagne. The next morning, he woke up with a hangover and realised he had spent £3,000. When he came to me, he was crushed by shame and remorse. Another patient did much the same in Portugal, except that one evening cost him £10,000. He got very drunk, bought everyone champagne and cocaine, gave away his pin number and he, too, was overwhelmed with shame. Another patient was sued by his wife. He had lost a fortune over the years on cocaine and sex workers. Now most of us are not likely to lose a couple of thousand pounds in one evening, but these stories illustrate the dangerous nature of these gateway substances. Sex and intoxicating substances make a dangerous combination.

You should, when thinking about your relapse prevention plan, consider any specific changes that might make an immediate difference. For example, it might be a good idea to reposition your computer so that the screen faces the doorway. If you use the computer at home, it could be placed in the family room rather than in the study or bedroom. It is possible to get software packages that will block pornography. Whatever you can do that will delay access to pornography or sex worker sites will give you more time to exit the behaviour. Another good idea is to go to bed with your partner and not stay up 'working' on the computer.

It might be a good idea to return to your provisional sex plan and see how useful it has been over the weeks since it was first assembled. How has it gone? What changes are needed? Does it need to be tightened up or loosened up? Very often, in drawing up a sex plan, there is a tendency to draw up counsels of perfection. Experience will dictate whether it has been drawn too loosely or too tightly. Your sex plan should reflect a considered, measured and, most importantly, realistic action plan for your sexual behaviour. Think again about the three categories of behaviour: 'OK', 'not OK' and 'iffy'. Sometimes, as one moves through recovery, the content of each box might change. Men in our groups will often move flirting to the 'not OK' box. Masturbation is a matter of choice and some men will keep it in the 'OK' box, while some will move it to the 'not OK' box. Other men will move masturbation using internet pornography into the 'not OK' box. The choice is yours. It is possible to get so used to onscreen sex that the real thing can lose its appeal. There can be difficulties in the relationship when there is a dispute between you and your partner over acceptable behaviour. This creates significant problems for an enduring relationship.

In Alcoholics Anonymous there is a saying that in recovery 'you have to change your friends'. The meaning of this is that if you continue to see people that have aided and abetted your acting out, you put yourself at risk. This is especially true if you are one of those people who is particularly sensitive to the views and thoughts of others. I had a patient who wanted to stop drinking alcohol but he could not bear the jokes and the pressure put on him by friends to have a drink. Something of the same applies to sexual acting out. Sometimes there are specific people who can lead you to act out, in the same way that there are people who can lead you to drink. These can be the men on a stag weekend, colleagues on a business trip or a friend with whom you used to have beer and cocaine. The beer and the cocaine might be, for you, the way into unwanted sexual behaviour. So it is probably right not to spend time with this friend or to see him or her in carefully controlled circumstances. It might make sense to make a list of your friends and write next to their names whether or not you have acted out with them or whether they have contributed to putting you in a place where you can act out. You could then consider whether you should go on seeing them and if so, under what circumstances and in what conditions it would be safe to see them. I had a patient who had put Sophie on his 'not to contact list'. After some months of internal struggle, he said to himself, 'I am going to see her'. Sophie was a girl with whom he often had sex and who used cocaine and crystal meth. He went to see her and, under the influence of cocaine, he used crystal meth. He fell asleep and then choked on his vomit. He was left brain damaged. This is an extreme story, but it is a cautionary tale about the harmful consequences of keeping company with the wrong people.

Equally, it might be worth making a list of people with whom it is good for you to spend time. They might include people from a sexual recovery programme. The fellowships provide a place where it is possible to make new friends who can encourage you and who have shared the same trials and tribulations. You might know someone at the office with whom it would be good for you spend time. Take a piece of paper and make a list of such people and give one of them a ring and suggest a coffee or lunch.

Not only is it wise to consider who you spend time with, you may also need to think about where you spend it. The cues for sexual acting out come from inside and outside. The inner ones are feeling states that are conducive to compulsive sexual behaviour, the outer cues are people, places, events and circumstances that are bring back memories or impressions of acting out. Just being in a situation that is reminiscent of acting out is enough to trigger the desire to act out. Strip clubs are generally not a good idea. If your acting out is combined with, or follows, alcohol, it might be best to avoid bars or restaurants where you used to drink. Another problem can be business trips. I have come across a number of men who have frequently been involved in sexual behaviour when they are on a business trip. The hotel bar might need to be avoided at the end of the day. Abroad more than in the United Kingdom, hotel bars are sometimes places chosen by sex workers. Some men who have acted out in the Marylebone area of London, where my clinic is located, will tell me that they feel triggered just coming into Marylebone because they have used sex workers around my office.

If you stop acting out, you will almost always hurt. This is best avoided by cultivating rich and meaningful activities to provide alternative ways of managing stress, or improving your self-image or reducing loneliness. Make a list of all sorts of things that you can think of that would be interesting alternatives. Earlier I referred to one patient of mine who used to act out on sex and drugs from Thursday to Sunday. He substituted a Spanish class on Thursday and interrupted the cycle of addiction. You might search the internet for hobbies, crafts, drawing classes, dance or sporting activities. Rich and meaningful activities build up your quality of life and the better your quality of life, the less you will need to leave it for sexual oblivion. After all, it is not really about sex. It is about an escape strategy from negative feeling states.

Another piece of equipment in the arsenal of recovery would be a Twelve Step Meeting. I will write more about these meetings later on in this book. You could go to a meeting of Sex Addicts Anonymous or to a meeting of Sex and Love Addicts Anonymous. You might find the meetings strange at first but, with a little perseverance, you would soon get the hang of the meeting formats. These meetings are built around the concept of a 'Higher Power' that is greater than you. A lot of people, especially in secular Britain, take the power of the meeting as their Higher Power. In any event, there is a slogan in Sex Addicts Anonymous, 'Take what you want and leave the rest', which allows anyone to be able to participate and, at the same time, hold on to their own positions. The notion of a Higher Power helps many sex addicts to realise that recovery is something that cannot be done on one's own. The widely held belief is that the starting point of addiction recovery is surrender: an admission that 'this is too big for me, I cannot do this, someone else has to take over'.

You also might consider whether individual psychotherapy might be a good idea. I have been in therapy for many years. I do not go to therapy in order to work on any particular issue, although life seems to throw up issues as I move towards the end of it. I go because I find it helpful to spend an hour talking about myself with someone who knows me and who I can trust has my best interests at heart. It could be important for some of you to get a better understanding of yourself. It is also possible in individual therapy to address some of the problems that drive addictive behaviour. Depression, anxiety and low self-esteem are all responsive to therapeutic treatment. I would strongly recommend individual therapy for anyone trying to recover from compulsive sexual behaviour. The use of therapy is manifold: it can be a place to be understood, a place to be heard and a place to gain understanding. It can be a place to address some of the problems that accompany and drive compulsive sexual behaviour.

If you are in a relationship, you will need to think about how to improve the quality of the relationship. Of course the best way to do that is to embark on a radical change of behaviour. This may take some time to put into effect and your partner is likely to be angry, mistrustful, shamed and indignant. It may take her months to come back to normal. In my experience, it is best to avoid staggered disclosures. By staggered, I mean a little now, and a little more next week; the result is that your partner wonders whether this will ever stop. It will take time to win back the confidence of your partner. She will be traumatised. You might spend more time with her. Work on your communication skills. It is a good idea to set aside time just for the two of you and maybe also spend more time doing family things. Give her time. It might help to go through this book with her or order books aimed at the partners of sexually compulsive men for her to read. It might give her some confidence if you are in a recovery fellowship. There is a programme, COSA, for the partners of sexually compulsive men. It is a non-professional gathering largely comprised of women, who meet together for support and for their own wellbeing. She might find it helpful. When the time seems right, you might go to relationship therapy together. We see many couples at our clinic and we are specialised in the particular help that is needed. Any good quality professional marriage and relationship therapist can help to put things back together again. It can provide a place to talk about hard issues in a safe and contained space. Whatever action you take, bear in mind that your partner will be overwhelmingly hurt. The person that she thought she could trust turns out to be untrustworthy. Sometimes there has been a long secret life and she might wonder whether she ever knew you.

While you are trying to put things right with your partner, it might be sensible to consider other people with whom you need to make amends. Making amends really just means giving an apology for harm done and having a formal opportunity to say 'sorry'. This is sometimes best done in person unless, on reflection, you feel that this might harm them further. It can be a letter or an email. Consider all the people you might have hurt during your time in addiction. Making amends is a painful process and done really not for them but for you. They are free to choose whether to accept the amends that you make. The outcome is not your business. Make the amends and accept the response with grace. Again, the making of amends is primarily an act of restitution that you might need to make. Once it is done, there is nothing more that can be done. I recommend in some cases, where you know that it would be inappropriate to make direct amends, to make symbolic amends. I have known men who have given money to charity as a symbolic amend.

Another important part of recovery and relapse prevention is giving service. This means being ready and willing to help the 'still suffering addict'. This can also be a way of changing the focus of your life away from yourself to other people. We all need connection with other people. Some say that addiction is 'self-will run riot'. You can do something as simple as making the tea and coffee at a Twelve Step Meeting or it can be bigger. Some take on a volunteer role in a charitable organisation; for example, I know a man who works one night a week in a soup kitchen. Whatever it is, the rendering of service is valuable. In serving others, we are served.

As we are come to the end of this chapter on relapse prevention, consider the specific choices that you need to make to change the way you live your life. Strive for the long term. Make healthy choices. Each person is different and each person has to put together an individualised relapse prevention plan. It should contain not only what you want to avoid but also the positive actions that might be available to you. One patient took a

French class, another took up dancing, another decided to increase his exercise programme, whilst another person decided to attend a weekly meeting of Sex Addicts Anonymous. Whatever you decide to do, make sure that the negative is balanced with the positive. If you just stop your compulsive sexual behaviour, you will hurt. It is the hurting that we then relieve with compulsive sexual behaviour, so make sure that your recovery plan includes the positive as well as the negative.

Exercise: relapse prevention worksheet

Answer the questions below and then write out a forward plan.

What are the triggers for my compulsive sexual behaviour?

_____

_____

_____

_____

_____

What emotional states make me vulnerable to compulsive sexual behaviour?

_____

_____

_____

_____

_____

What substances tend to be a gateway into sexually compulsive behaviour?

_____

_____

_____

_____

What specific short-term changes can I make to help me break my addictive cycle?

_____

_____

_____

_____

_____

What sexual behaviour is definitely off-limits for me?

_____

_____

_____

_____

_____

What behaviours make me more likely to act out sexually?

_____

_____

_____

_____

_____

What sexual behaviours are good for me and give me peace of mind?

_____

_____

_____

_____

_____

What activities nurture me and build me up: physically, mentally, emotionally and spiritually?

_____

_____

_____

_____

_____

What activities do not build me up, that I would prefer to limit or stop?

_____

_____

_____

_____

Who are the people to avoid, with whom I have acted out before or have given me permission to act out?

_____

_____

_____

_____

What friendships should I cultivate that reinforce my wellbeing and my sense of adequacy?

_____

_____

_____

_____

How would Sex Addicts Anonymous or Sex and Love Addicts Anonymous help me in my recovery?

_____

_____

_____

_____

_____

What advantages might there be in individual psychotherapy?

_____

_____

_____

_____

_____

What can I do to improve the quality of my relationship with loved ones?

_____

_____

_____

_____

_____

To whom do I need to apologise and make amends?

_____

_____

_____

_____

_____

What specific choices do I need to make in order to remain on the road to sexual recovery?

_____

_____

_____

_____

_____

Having answered these questions, it would be a good idea to create a relapse prevention plan and write it out on a card.

Here is a sample plan:

Daily:

* Read one page of a recovery book.
* Read from a daily meditation book.
* Phone one friend.

Weekly:

* Run three times a week.
* Take one walk a week with the children.
* See my psychotherapist.
* Go to one meeting of Sex Addicts Anonymous.

Monthly:

* Take my partner out to dinner, just the two of us.

Annually:

* Go on a retreat.

Now, write out your own plan.

Daily

_____

_____

_____

_____

_____

Weekly

_____

_____

_____

_____

_____

Monthly

_____

_____

_____

_____

_____

Annually

_____

_____

_____

_____

_____

Make your plan realistic. It is possible to get carried away and make a plan that will be impossible to keep. If you do not stick to your plan, maybe revise it or just get back to the plan once you realise that you have slipped. After all, you are trying to make a big change of behaviour and such a change requires dedication and ongoing commitment. The more you return to the plan, the easier it will become.

Recap of tasks for week 10

• Answer the questions in the Relapse Prevention Worksheet.
• Write your Relapse Prevention Plan on a card and keep it with you.
• Continue to keep the urge diary.
• Recite Pillar 10 three times a day.

Pillar for week 10

I look to the future. I have looked at my compulsive sexual behaviour. I have tried to understand it. Now I resolve to go onwards. This is the beginning of the end and the end of the beginning. I will take the road less travelled. I am making the journey from shame to grace.

This week's learning summary:

_____

_____

_____

_____

_____

_____

_____

_____

_____

_____

Part III

Ancillary readings

Chapter 8

Internet pornography

In the early days of this clinic, a man came to me with a problem with internet pornography. This is his story. He temporarily lived and worked in France and came home to his wife once a month. He worked in an Anglo-French publishing house as an IT expert. He told me that when the week ended on Friday, he would go online and watch pornography until late in the evening, then continue all day Saturday and Sunday. On Monday morning, he would get up to go to work feeling exhausted and despicable. He would ruminate that he had wasted two days and three evenings doing nothing but looking at pornography. During the week he would knuckle down and get on with life but every weekend the same pattern of behaviour kept repeating. He also found that he would get tired of just watching video clips of people having sex and would range further and further into the fringes of the internet for extra erotic stimulation. His wife knew nothing of his secret life. This whole process was undermining his confidence and destroying his self-esteem. Unfortunately, the internet can become a downward spiral pulling you further and further into an online presence and an offline absence.

I am not opposed to the internet. It would be impossible to function in the modern world without its use. I could not manage life without email correspondence and the ability to carry out research on topics of interest. You can easily buy books, download music and films, as well as get news and weather information. Sexual minorities and those living in isolated communities can connect with others through the internet. There are websites dedicated to the special interests of the lesbian and gay community, BDSM websites, as well as websites providing information and services for transsexuals. Marginalised and stigmatised individuals can find a supportive community and an end to isolation. Similarly, the internet provides information and guidance that helps individuals to protect themselves against HIV/AIDS and other sexually transmitted infections. There is much good about the internet and I do not support the tendency to attribute all evil in the sexual realm to the expansion of the internet. I do not support any ban on internet pornography or on the use of the internet to provide sexual services to those who want to use them. However, like almost any good thing, it comes with a bad side and the bad side is its availability as an escape from life's problems, rather than a solution to these problems.

Internet gaming addiction is described as a new category for 'further study' in the most recent publication of the *Diagnostic Manual* of the American Psychiatric Association (APA 2013). This manual is the standard classification of mental disorders used by mental health professionals. Near to this designation is a note about sexual addiction, which concludes that there is not sufficient peer-reviewed information for it to be included as a mental disorder (APA 2013). That does not mean that sexual addiction does not exist. It means that there is not enough peer-reviewed information available to warrant its formal classification. In any event, I am not convinced that it is a 'mental disorder'; nevertheless, problematic sexual behaviour, whether it is called an addiction or not, is real, troublesome and potentially destructive.

Pornography originally meant 'writings about harlots'. It would be more accurate now for us to define it as the provision of explicit material for the purpose of sexual arousal. Because the internet is developing so fast, it is quite impossible to provide up-to-date information on the statistics; within a week, they become out of date. The most recent information that I have is as follows:

- 68 million web searches are carried out daily in the United States alone.
- In 2010, 13 per cent of all global web searches were for pornography.
- 10 per cent of adults admit to having an addiction to online pornography.
- Pornography websites have larger revenues than the top technology companies combined (Microsoft, Google, Amazon, eBay, Yahoo, Apple and Netflix).

(Stop Porn Culture 2014)

Research over the past few years has suggested that internet sexual addiction is a new and often unrecognised problem with a number of social, economic and occupational consequences. One of the problems with consistent use of internet pornography, returning to the principle of supernormal stimuli, is that it changes our perception of real women. You can get so used to looking at women with very large breasts, keen on lots of casual sex, that it distorts the reality of women. It is easy to see how constant use of pornography can diminish the sexual attractiveness of a real woman. The brain's mirror neurons allow us to feel what another is feeling. If you see someone crying, you will usually be moved to wonder, or even ask, if they are alright or need any help. These mirror neurons help us to resonate with the feelings that we see and allow us to respond in appropriately empathic ways. Mirror neurons also work when we look at pictures of arousal. When we see pictures of men and women aroused, that can create arousal in us as well.

The internet can also be used to avoid life's problems. One of the paradoxical outcomes of internet use is that, while it can be an escape from loneliness, research has shown that it can increase social isolation and self-alienation (Chaney and Chang 2005). Maltz and Maltz (2008) claim that the overuse of internet pornography can cause boredom, isolation, objectification of others, low self-worth and sexual addiction.

I think another problem with overuse of the internet is that you can become bored with routine pornography, and therefore the direction of the search can become more and more unusual or even extreme and there is an escalation in the amount of time spent online. There is endless novelty on the internet. I think this means that if you have a recessive sexual script for, let's say, redheads or amputees, it can be brought into the forefront of your sexual template as it is reinforced through masturbation and the power of the orgasm. According to one researcher (Young 2007), overuse of the internet can cause changes in offline sexual behaviour, usually in terms of a reduced interest in sexual behaviour with the partner. A large number of men have reported other sexual problems as well as relationship problems accompanying internet pornography addiction. However, I am not sure which comes first. Just because two things occur side-by-side does not mean that one causes the other. A number of other researchers have suggested that internet porn use is often accompanied by loneliness, depression, academic and marital problems, missed opportunities, excessive expenditure, reduced self-care and other social problems (Ceyhan and Ceyhan 2008; Van Rooij et al. 2012; Yen et al. 2007). Lost time is the greatest individual loss that accompanies internet pornography addiction.

A large number of men attend our groups in an attempt to save their relationships. Sexual addiction injures the partner and destabilises the relationship. There is often a catastrophic loss of trust from the partner in the relationship. The use of internet pornography inherently attacks the well-being of the relationship. Over and over, I have heard women cry out pitifully 'How can I ever trust him again?' I have found that the men are themselves devastated by a recognition of the consequences of their sexual addiction. Given the attraction of internet pornography, women can feel demeaned, unattractive and undesired. The result can be just as powerful as the discovery of a secret affair. Internet pornography addiction has the capacity to break hearts and destroy relationships.

Earlier in this book I have written about your core belief. Most sex addicts have a core belief of 'I am not good' and with that comes the horrible feeling of shame. The feeling of shame seems intolerable and internet pornography is used to escape the feeling of shame. However, this only works as a short-term strategy because the use of internet pornography further confirms the notion that 'I am not good' and this sets in motion a dreadful cycle: shame, internet sex, more shame and then more internet sex.

This section has taken a closer look at internet pornography addiction. While accepting that the internet is here to stay and that normal life would not really be possible without recourse to it, we have noted some of the problems associated with the addictive use of internet pornography. Some take the view that it can modify sexual templates. Others have cautioned that, paradoxically, it is used to escape loneliness but at the same time increases loneliness. We have noted as well that the use of internet pornography can have a distressing and disrupting impact on the quality and endurance of relationships. Although a cheap (unless you use webcams) and relatively safe way to act out sexually, its use can have far-reaching implications for the user and their loved ones.

Chapter 9

Quirky sexual practices

I was once asked to give evidence as an expert witness at a murder trial. The defendant was found guilty of murder and sentenced to 20 years in prison. He did actually kill the woman but I am not persuaded that he intended to murder her. They were involved in 'knife play' and he was terribly drunk. His hand slipped and she died. It did not help his case that he was heard in the garden, that same afternoon, shouting, 'I will kill you, you bitch'.

Now, most of you are not into knife play or breath play. These would be located at the extreme end of what might be considered quirky. So I will not much devote much space to writing about these topics here. Auto-asphyxiation is another dangerous practice, which should be done with the utmost care, if at all; be extremely cautious, it is easy to kill yourself accidently. Most of the quirky sexual practices that I want to address here involve domination/submission, cross-dressing or some refinements on these themes. Anything which is exploitative and coercive is clearly legally and morally wrong. So I am going to stay with behaviours that involve consenting adults and that are not illegal or immoral. If your behaviours stray into the coercive and abusive, I would suggest that you immediately ring up a skilled psychosexual therapist to help you deal with these problems. In the UK, the Lucy Faithfull Foundation has a helpline called 'Stop It Now', which can be a very useful centre of help. Our clinic has a forensic specialist who can carry out risk assessments, as well as provide treatment. Whatever you do, if you are even tempted to do something coercive or abusive, you need to get help with this quickly.

Domination and submission are common quirky behaviours, which are widespread in the population. If you are into BDSM, you are certainly not alone. It is estimated that between 1 and 5 per cent of the American and Australian populations are involved in BDSM (Critelli and Bivona 2008). Professor Brett Kahr, a leading psychotherapist, wrote *Sex and the Psyche*

(2007), a book based on a YouGov survey of 15,000 people in Great Britain. The survey found that 4 per cent of Britons had fantasies about being violent towards someone and 6 per cent had fantasies of violence being practised upon them. I am quoting these figures in order to convey that this might be a minority sexual interest but it is a sizeable minority. Furthermore, there is a significant body of opinion that would argue that sexual sadism and sexual masochism have not been found to be correlated with psychological ill health. In fact, people involved in these practices have shown good evidence of having a somewhat higher level of social and psychological functioning, as measured by educational levels, income and occupational status, when compared with the rest of the population. BDSM does not appear to be part of a deviant lifestyle and BDSM practitioners are 'surprisingly' normal.

However, if you are into BDSM or rough sex, please be careful. Agree scenarios in advance, agree safe words, use the traffic light system ('red' for stop, 'yellow' for caution and 'green' for press ahead). Never practise risky behaviours under the influence of alcohol or recreational drugs. These substances shut down your judgement and impair your cognitive functions, easily turning sex into a dangerous event.

Quirky sexual behaviour is technically called a 'paraphilia'. It is not listed as a medical problem in the latest edition of the *Diagnostic and Statistical Manual* of the American Psychiatric Society unless it causes overwhelming distress or severe life problems. The word *paraphilia* comes from the Greek *para* meaning 'alongside of' and *philia* meaning 'love'. These sexual patterns are set up in childhood and tend to come to life with sexual maturity. They are normally the result of some deprivation or trauma in the childhood situation. By trauma, I do not mean some terrible act of violence but rather something less, but repetitive. It is a particular problem when there is an alcoholic parent or a parent who is mentally ill. Not everyone with that kind of family background will develop a quirky sexual script but some do and the meaning is hidden in the act. If you take the sex out of it, it will reveal itself. So if someone wants to spank women, take the sex out of it and it will give you the meaning: it is the punishment of women, usually set up in unconscious resentment towards a punishing mother.

Most of the authorities that I have consulted (Bader 2008; Kahr 2007; Money 1986; Stoller 1975) agree that fantasy and quirky scripts are an encoding of trauma, resulting in eroticisation and triumph. The deficits, traumas and humiliations of childhood are made pleasurable and changed into mastery and triumph. The unbearable is made bearable. Whatever quirk you have, bear in mind that you did not ask for it. It was set up in your developmental history and you have no choice in having it. You do, though, have a choice in what you do about it and whether you act upon it. If you do not want the quirky script, or if the script hinders and harms your relationships, then you have a problem. In so far as the paraphilia is involved in the addictive process, when the addictive process is left behind, the power of the paraphilia diminishes. There are also a number of ways suggested to reduce or remove the paraphilia. These all involve some form of aversion therapy. In aversion therapy, the paraphilia is paired with an unpleasant stimulus and this pairing is said to lead to a reduction in the erotic power of the paraphilia. Some authorities recommend this process, while others are not convinced that it has any lasting effects. I think that this debate is set to continue. The use of aversion therapy is problematic. Some would even question whether it is an ethical process. It is certainly a hard process and the fall-out rates are very high. It is rarely used for a 'normal quirky script' and tends to be limited to those with scripts that are dangerous. I have only used a form of aversion therapy twice. Once was with a man who exhibited himself on the bus going to work. I gave him a vial of smelling salts to use to interrupt the process. It did not work. The second time I used it was with a man who would pay women to do degrading things to him. At the end of each experience with one of these sex workers, the man would be suicidal. It did not work for this man either. He finally went into residential treatment and, the last time I heard from him, he had had seven months of total abstinence. For him, residential treatment revolutionised his life. It cost him and his family a great deal of money but he has a new life. It was a very hard road but the outcome has been successful. The life he used to have was filled with misery; now this has been transformed into a life filled with peace.

Alongside most quirky scripts, there can be a range of problems. These include mood disorders, substance abuse problems, depression and high levels of anxiety. Some would say that the best treatment for an unwanted quirky script is a combination of group work, individual work and medication. It is well known that the anti-depressant medications selective serotonin reuptake inhibitors (SSRIs) frequently reduce sexual need and desire. This combined process is generally regarded as the optimum treatment plan. Outcomes are best in this combined therapeutic process when there is early treatment, a strong sense of self, high levels of motivation and a substantial part of the sexual template that includes normal sexual functioning.

I started this chapter by writing about a murder trial; I will finish with the same trial. The man had been drinking spirits for two days solid. He phoned up an old sexual partner and invited her over. It is said that she enjoyed 'rough sex'. They had sex a number of times during the night. In the early morning, they went down to the kitchen to get a knife for knife play. He was so drunk that his hand slipped and he cut her throat and she bled to death. He then blacked out next to her body for eight hours. He turned himself in to the police the next day. Neither of them would have known one of the rules around knife play: never do it when intoxicated. It is, as we can see in this case, dangerous, with lethal consequences.

This week's learning summary:

_____

_____

_____

_____

_____

_____

_____

_____

_____

_____

Chapter 10

Cross addictions and comorbid disorders

Introduction

Sexual addiction can be accompanied by a number of additional problems. These can include so-called 'cross addictions', where the sexual addiction is combined with one or more other addictive processes. Sexual addiction can also be accompanied by mood problems, such as depression, anxiety, shame and loneliness. In addition, there can sometimes be a problematic dynamic in your relationship with your partner that contributes to your need to act out sexually. This is not to blame the partner. The dynamic is usually 'out of awareness'. It exists but cannot be readily seen. This chapter will explore and comment on both cross addictions and mood problems that often accompany compulsive sexual behaviour.

Cross addictions

Research has made it clear that compulsive sexual behaviour is often combined with the use of alcohol and other recreational drugs. Some research suggests that 40–60 per cent of sex addicts also have a substance use problem. The high prevalence of this combination suggests that both the sexual behaviour and the substance problem have the same root.

The biggest offender is alcohol. I have patients who only ever act out under the influence of alcohol. Perhaps 30 per cent of my patients use alcohol to excess and some then pay for sex workers. Alcohol disinhibits and cuts you off from your cognitive mind. We do and say things under the influence of alcohol that we would never do or say if we were sober. After a couple of beers, the future and the past disappear. All thoughts of the consequence go out the window. Alcohol is a mood-altering substance. The disinhibition also can cause a person to make bad decisions and take unwise action.

Perhaps more difficult than alcohol is the use of cocaine. Every man who has joined our treatment programme who uses cocaine has dropped out after two or three sessions. This leads me to believe that if you have a cocaine problem, you should deal with that first before focusing on compulsive sexual behaviour. Cocaine so radically alters brain chemistry that, in my view, it must be left behind. It is a dangerous drug that does a great deal of damage to the brain. The impact of the high is so great that one can become addicted in one use only. It increases the risk of a heart attack or a stroke. When started in adolescence, it has long-lasting implications for our ability to think and our emotional functioning. Cocaine can be a particular problem for men who use sex workers. Some sex workers supply cocaine and are, themselves, addicted to its use. It is easy to see the road to ruin: a few drinks disinhibit and lead to a visit to a sex worker, who then suggests to the disinhibited man that a line or two of cocaine would be a good idea, to enhance the erotic pleasure.

Addictions do not just sit side-by-side. They interact in different ways. The example at the end of the paragraph above suggests one way addictions interact and that is known as 'fusion'. Another combination is when one addiction pops up to replace another. Anyone who has tried to give up smoking will know this one. If you stop smoking, you start eating. One addiction, such as alcohol, can be used to excuse another. It can also be that one addiction is part of a ritual that leads to another. As you can see, addictions are a complex and interconnected phenomenon.

With behavioural addictions, the behaviour is used to anaesthetise the negative feeling state, rather than a substance. The behaviour increases dopamine in the brain. This is true, for example, of 'romance addiction'. Some research has been done on being in love and this research suggests that the process has the same effects as the use of a substance. Even shopping can be an addiction. I am used to running and I know that if I leave it for a few days, my body tells me something is wrong. I go for a run and feel good afterwards. The body produces sexual chemistry and each of us has a mandate to be sexual. In considering sexual behaviours, it is difficult to work out whether the urge is simply a response to the ebb and flow of your body's chemistry or whether the sexual desire is prompted by the need to anaesthetise a negative feeling state. This is a complicated decision-making process but as you become increasingly aware of the antecedents to compulsive sexual behaviour, it is possible to distinguish the difference.

Work can be another compulsive behaviour, creating what people call 'workaholics'. This is a behaviour that can have very good professional outcomes and is often highly rewarded. But, it is more than just being diligent at work. It is a complete disappearance into work as an escape from intolerable feeling states. This is especially true for men. Male identity is deeply tied up with professional life. When you know someone's profession or work life, you can fit them into a category of value. Once the professional identity is established, you will already have in mind background, education, class and their place in the social hierarchy. Some people have a touch of Obsessive Compulsive Disorder, which adds further to their commitment to the demands of work. Although workaholics can be successful in their chosen career, it has a serious downside. An agreeable work-life balance is important in the process of recovery from compulsive sexual behaviour. Over and over, I hear from patients that their fathers were never at home. Good parenting requires a balanced commitment of time. It is a problem to escape into work to avoid the intolerable feelings states and therefore neglect important family responsibilities, marital relationships and recreational activities. A good recovery usually means cultivating a balanced life, in which work, recreation, relaxation, sports and family commitments all find their rightful place.

Another interesting addictive process is involvement in religious activity. Now I am not saying that all religious people are addicts or that religion is an addictive process. To say such a thing would be very simplistic and deny the huge benefits of religious behaviour to the social order and to the individual religious person. That said, religion can be an alternative addictive process. Religious commitment can be a behavioural substitute to shore up a broken sense of self, to provide activities that can make the unbearable bearable. I have often seen in religious people a great deal of self-hatred that is transformed into prejudice and intolerance. For the shame-based person, religion can be a way of hiding the reality of the unloved self and sometimes accompanies sexual addiction. When it accompanies sexual addiction, this puts the person in between a rock and a hard place. The message of religion is often a shaming message. When the shame becomes unbearable, some resort to compulsive sexual behaviour. This, in turn, confirms the belief that they are shameful. So it goes on in an endless cycle. Some find their escape mechanisms from the sense of a defective self in both religion and sex. This is a very painful and destructive combination.

There are other cross addictions that I have not written about: compulsive eating as a pain reliever, gambling as an escape into excitement from the mundane and the pursuit of high adrenalin activities like sky diving, bungee jumping and motorcycle racing. I often think that gamblers are addicted to losing. Gambling is a highly exciting activity that brings with it a great deal more loss than gain. Using food as a pain reliever adds to the sense of defectiveness. In our world, people who are slim are socially valued and people who are fat can be treated with contempt. The high adrenalin activities can be dangerous and potentially lethal. In most of the recovery groups that we run, we see this whole range of cross addictions. In an average group of ten men, there will be one who gambles, several who use alcohol as the gateway into compulsive sexual behaviour, one or two who use cocaine, one or two who medicate themselves with food, two or three who use religion and a couple of men who are workaholics. Often several of these behaviours turn up in the same person.

Mood problems

Mood problems frequently accompany compulsive sexual behaviour. However, it is not possible to conclude that, just because two things are side-by-side, one necessarily causes the other. In the case of sexual addiction, the evidence points to the fact that compulsive sexual behaviour is an escape from the difficult feelings of mood. It suggests to me also that mood problems are intrinsically linked to sexually compulsive behaviour. The mood problems that we are considering are:

- depression
- loneliness
- anxiety
- shame
- boredom proneness.

While these are not all disorders, they are all painful feeling states. As we know already, compulsive sexual behaviour is simply an attempt to escape one of these feeling states. Kafka (1991), writing in the *Journal of Clinical Psychiatry*, describes sexual addiction as a 'sexual regulation disorder in comorbid association with a mood disorder' (Kafka 1991: 63). 'Comorbid' simply means two symptoms presenting together. I would probably rewrite this as 'a pattern of sexual behaviour which presents with problematic mood states'. The term 'disorder' seems to be too medical and has the tendency to turn both sex and moods into a pathology.

In cases of severe depression, it is important to get the mood state treated as early as possible. Depression robs you of motivation and motivation is important to overcoming sexual addiction. It creates disincentives to do anything and the less you do, the more depressed you become. It also sets up negative thinking and the negative thinking contributes to the problem. Depression can be treated with anti-depressant medication and/or cognitive behavioural therapy. CBT might be the preferred route for those who do not want to take medication. CBT has another advantage over medication. You would learn techniques that can be used in future times should the problem reoccur. If you think you are depressed, you should get help. Depression can be treated.

In our recovery groups, there are usually a couple of people who are beset by loneliness. These are 'in-built' problems and bear no relationship to having a partner, a football team or a golfing associate. Something happened in the childhood development which leaves the person feeling lonely almost all the time. People who act out sexually on loneliness are often terribly afraid of being abandoned. Loneliness often accompanies sexual addiction and, in particular, internet sexual addiction. One tries to solve the loneliness problem online but that sets up deeper and genuine loneliness.

In our treatment programme, large numbers of men have come to realise that their sexual acting out is closely related to high levels of anxiety. They have come to realise that they use sexual behaviour to escape high levels of stress. It is important to relieve the stress so that the tendency to act out sexually diminishes. Sometime there is a constant and debilitating level of stress and I would recommend that you see a cognitive behavioural therapist to get help with this. Such a condition is known as Generalised Anxiety Disorder. We would use this term when the anxiety levels are so high that they actually prevent normal living. There are a whole range of techniques available to help reduce anxiety and, once learned, they can be employed in the future to sustain anxiety reduction.

As we saw earlier in this book, shame is the feeling that one is unacceptable, unworthy, intrinsically flawed, diminished, unlovable, humiliated and, therefore, a potential victim of rejection with the loss of all human dignity. While shame is not a medical disorder, it is a profoundly painful experience. Many people are shame-based. That means that underneath an attitude of confidence and effectiveness, there is a continuous, often unacknowledged, base of shame. Human beings are hardwired to be in connection with others and threats to this human connectedness are powerfully disturbing. Most sex addicts that I have dealt with have high levels of toxic shame. You can momentarily escape from this feeling of shame by sexual behaviour but afterwards the shame is intensified. The shame is relieved by sexual behaviour but, at the same time, it sets up further shame. You must be a bad person because you wasted time on internet pornography or you use sex workers on business trips. Shame is both relieved temporarily and intensified in the long term with sexual acting out.

In my clinical work, I have come across a category of men who seem to have a need for higher levels of stimulation than do others. I call these men 'boredom prone' or 'boredom intolerant'. It is as though their boredom gauge is set lower than the rest of us. They seem to require abnormally high levels of excitement to feel truly alive. In such cases, I suggest that they learn to celebrate the simple and the ordinary. There is great beauty in the ordinary. You just have to notice it.

Conclusion

In this chapter, we have looked at cross addictions and accompanying mood problems. Both of these can lead to sexual acting out. Sexual addiction is not so much about sex as it is a mechanism to relieve one of these feeling states or mood problems. Cross addictions are frequently gateway substances to sexual addiction. If you really want a good and complete recovery, you would do well to consider how these factors are involved with your sexual behaviour. Ultimately, a good recovery is best sustained on a platform of wellness. If you feel well and are content with life, then there is no need to escape into sex as way of avoiding the unpleasant. Sex can then become an enjoyable recreational activity or an important facilitator of intimacy in a relationship.

This week's learning summary:

_____

_____

_____

_____

_____

_____

_____

_____

_____

_____

Chapter 11

Group work

Whilst this is a self-help book, many people find that the only reliable way to sustain recovery is with help from another person or people. If you do not get the help you need from this book or if you find that you keep slipping back into the old behaviour in spite of all your good intentions to change, then you could give group work a try. As there are high levels of secrecy and shame around sexual behaviour, this might sound like an unappealing prospect. However, if you do not get the sobriety that you are hoping for on your own, you could bite the bullet and get a group or another person's involvement to help you move forward.

Another idea is to go into individual therapy. You do not need the most expensive or the most highly qualified person for you to benefit from individual therapy. Just make sure that you like the therapist and that you have a sense of confidence in their understanding and level of skill. I understand that it is not good manners to shop around but I do not see why this should be a problem. Obviously, you would need to have one session before you would be able to make up your mind. If the first person does not seem quite right, try a couple more until you hit on exactly the right person. I had one therapist that really got me exactly and it was wonderful to be able to see her and to know that she understood. She died during the time I was seeing her and, all day, I wandered around singing the spiritual song 'Sometimes I feel like a motherless child'. Having a good relationship with a therapist relieves isolation and can reduce loneliness.

In my view, there are two kinds of therapy. One is cognitive behavioural therapy, which is based upon the implementation of evidence-based protocols to help with specific disorders, while the other is a more general exploration into the construction of the self. If you are aiming to relieve one of the problems mentioned in the last section, I would suggest a cognitive behavioural therapist, but if you are looking for self-awareness, I would choose a general psychotherapist. Some are more non-directive than others so bear this in mind when considering who you might see. One word of caution: it is difficult to leave unwanted sexual behaviour behind with just individual therapy. Individual therapy should be used to augment other recovery work. If you are using this book to move forward, it can be a considerable help to have someone alongside you in this process. In this case, give the therapist a copy of the book as you work through it.

Sexual recovery fellowship groups are free to attend and are not led by professionals. They are made up of recovering addicts working together, sharing their trials, tribulations and failures, as well as their successes, hopes and victories in the process of recovery. It is entirely a peer-to-peer process. This has some advantages over working with a person who is a paid professional. As it is a self-help programme, all are equal and each contribution to the group process can be of value. There is greater diversity of input from these programmes. They are all based on the model that was set up in 1935 with the foundation of Alcoholics Anonymous. While these programmes are theistic and normally involve a belief in God, this should not really be a problem for the non-believer. The focus is upon the idea of the submission of the self to a Higher Power. In secular Britain, the group, or the programme itself, is taken as the Higher Power. In a nutshell, each group involves a Twelve Step process that can be summarised into the following components: surrender to a Higher Power, a moral inventory, the making of amendments to those harmed and a continuation in this process throughout life. The last step is focused on helping others in the same condition. Even if you are put off by the 'God' language of the Twelve Steps, you should bear in mind an important slogan: 'Take what you want and leave the rest'. With this slogan in mind, anyone can benefit from an involvement in a Twelve Step Sexual Recovery Group.

The sexual recovery fellowships that currently operate in the United Kingdom are Sexaholics Anonymous (SA), Sex Addicts Anonymous (SAA) and Sex and Love Addicts Anonymous (SLAA). These were first established in London and then spread throughout the country. It is possible to attend meetings all over the world. Different fellowships meet at different times and days of the week. It is possible to augment one's recovery by attending one of these on a regular basis.

Sexaholics Anonymous (SA) has a shared bottom line that one under-takes no sex with self or another outside of heterosexual marriage. This seems, to me, to be structurally homophobic. However, I have been assured by a long-standing member of SA that it is not homophobic and that gay people are well-represented in the membership because of its focus on 'progressive victory over lust'.

Sex Addicts Anonymous (SAA) is a largely male fellowship. There are women who attend but not in great numbers. In this fellowship, each individual sets his/her own bottom line. In other words, you work to a personal sex plan and work towards your own definition of sobriety. The definition of abstinence is self-defined. This seems to me to be a genuinely inclusive fellowship and might be a useful addition to your own recovery process.

The last sexual recovery fellowship to be considered is Sex and Love Addicts Anonymous (SLAA). Because of its inclusion of 'love' in the title, around half the participants are women. SLAA includes the HOW programme (Honest, Open and Willing), a demanding and austere recovery programme. I have had a small number of patients who have been through it and all have found it helpful. In each case these were people whose addiction had made their life utterly unmanageable.

I believe that Twelve Step programmes are effective because they are group-based. The group relieves the sense that one is alone, provides connected fellowship and imparts information. They also operate a system of sponsorship. This means that most group members take a sponsor who acts as an accountability partner and who helps to guide them through the programme and into recovery. But Twelve Step programmes also have their limitations. You have to go to a lot of meetings. The 'God' language can be off-putting for some. There is little in the programme about the neuroscience of addiction, little analysis of the addictive cycle, nothing on thinking errors and nothing specific on the family of origin. Despite these drawbacks, I would still recommend it for the recovering sexual addict. It is another tool that can be used on the road to recovery. Long ago, these were the only treatment programmes available in the United Kingdom. When all is said and done, they are effective programmes for the resolution of sexual addiction.

I personally started all the training programmes in the United Kingdom on recovery from sexual addiction. I also started all the programmes to train men and women to work with the problem of sexual addiction. Two or three people who originally trained with me have now created their own programmes. These will have evolved in distinctive ways and, having never been treated by my colleagues, I am not in a position to comment on the content or effectiveness of the work. They are people who I respect and I value their commitment to men and women affected by sexual addiction. I think that almost any specialist sexual recovery programme would be a useful adjunct to the work of recovery.

Our own programme at the Marylebone Centre is divided into three parts. Each part is 12 weeks long and meets on a weekday evening for two hours. The first part of the programme uses all the interventions for sexually addictive behaviour, while the second part continues this in a more informal way and goes more deeply into the issues. The third part of the programme is called 'The Restoration of Self-Esteem' and uses cognitive behavioural exercises to improve self-esteem. We have an excellent recovery rate. If you do not get the results you are looking for from this book, you might join a recovery fellowship or enrol on one of the specialised treatment programmes that operate around the country.

Finally, if the problem is overwhelming, disruptive or dangerous to yourself and others, you might need to go into residential treatment. There are a number of residential services that advertise that they work with sexual addiction. I would want to know exactly what they mean by this and exactly the kind of treatment they offer. At the moment, I would not promote any UK-based residential facility for the treatment of sexual addiction. No doubt, with time, this will change. There are expensive places in the United States that do this work effectively. I am told that good work goes on in South Africa. If this is true, South Africa is a much cheaper option that the States. For most men, residential treatment is not necessary and a non-residential programme is effective.

Group work can be a useful addition to individual recovery work. This could be the Twelve Step programmes which are free of charge or you could pay for a specialised programme. See how you get on with the exercises in this book. You can always access a free programme or a specialised treatment programme if the need arises.

Earlier on in this book, I made the statement that 'it is only a problem, if it is a problem'. If your sexual behaviour is not a problem to you, no one else should label it as sexual addiction. You are the only one who can determine whether or not it is a problem. However, if you are caught up in a pattern of sexual behaviour that causes you real distress, this book should help you bring the behaviour under control. If you are bothered by the amount of time you spend looking at internet pornography or the amount of money you are spending on sex workers, the exercises in this book will help you make some fundamental changes in your patterns of behaviour. However, if none of these things are a problem to you, then so be it.

This week's learning summary:

_____

_____

_____

_____

_____

_____

_____

_____

_____

_____

Conclusion

There are a number of arguments against the notion of sexual addiction. Some people think that an addiction must involve ingested substances. Recent studies in neuroscience are making this view out of date. We have become aware that certain activities can affect the brain chemistry in much the same way as recreational drugs. The brain chemistry of romantic attraction is a good example. It has all the characteristics of the effect of drugs of choice. For some people, exercise becomes an addictive process. For others it is food or shopping. Whatever the process, dopamine is released in the brain and dopamine is a key ingredient of pleasure. We can come to miss the dopamine high and seek to repeat it in distinctive ways.

Another perhaps more important argument is that the concept of sexual addiction turns sexuality itself into a pathology. At least, some forms of sexuality are pathologised. These are value judgements in the guise of psychology or medicine, for example that unless your behaviour is heteronormative, there is something wrong with it. As we do not choose our sexual templates, it does not seem fair to place some in the 'OK box' and others in the 'not OK' box. The exception to this is a sexual involvement that is coercive or with those who are unable to give consent. This would include children and the severely disabled or those whose decision-making is impaired by drugs or alcohol.

The one argument that I find the most convincing is that the sexual addiction narrative is just a narrative. The recent clamour around sexual addiction arose in the United States. Rugged individualism is a prominent feature in American society and sexual addiction recovery fits this narrative. A second feature is that it is a society in which there is much technological advancement. The underlying theme behind addiction recovery is that it moves towards balance and harmony by a 'technology of the self'. This term means that the self is an object of inspection and correction. While I have used the term sexual addiction in this book, it is really more about problematic sexual behaviour. By that I mean a pattern of sexual behaviour which gives you problems and reduces the overall quality of your life. I accept the terminology of addiction because it provides a useful overall framework for understanding and changing problematic sexual behaviours.

Human sexual behaviours and sexual templates have a wide range of variations. As I have said repeatedly, we do not ask for them. Just because you are into BDSM or cross-dressing, this should not be taken as a problem unless it is a problem to you. For example, you might just not like it, it might take up too much time or it might take you to dangerous places. You might be fine with it, but perhaps it is a turn-off to your partner. One of the problems with a quirky sexual script is that it is often hard to find a partner who wants to do the same thing. The things that you consider to be the height of sexual pleasure may be deeply unpleasant for someone else. If the disgust response is triggered, it is visceral in its impact and is seldom available for thoughtful, calm reflection.

One of the things that has come out in my study of sexual addiction is the tendency to turn male sexuality into a pathology. Male sexuality is linear, targeted and extremely powerful. Men are attracted and women attract. This is just the way it is. Women who are good at attracting improve their reproductive strategy. Men who are good at noticing women improve their reproductive strategy. To notice and be noticed has an important place in the overall human reproductive strategy.

One last feature to examine before closing is the tendency to stigmatise and ridicule those whose sexual scripts do not match the hetero-normative. There is a clear prejudice against sexual minorities. Western culture deeply discriminates against people with alternative sexual scripts. There has been a long tradition in the West of placing sexuality within a punitive framework. The prevailing Judeo-Christian culture continues to do this. The Church, the media, the political class and the elite do this with impunity. I believe that we must speak out against this stigmatisation and marginalisation of sexual minorities.

I hope that this workbook has made a small contribution to you, so that you, too, will experience freedom and happiness.

Resources

General

Birchard, T. (2015) *CBT for Compulsive Sexual Behaviour: A Guide for Professionals*, London: Routledge.

Bradshaw, J. (2005) *Healing the Shame that Binds You*, Deerfield Beach, FA: Health Communications, Inc.

Carnes, P. (1991) *Don't Call It Love*, New York: Bantam Books.

Carnes, P. (2001) *Out of the Shadows: Understanding Sex Addiction*, Center City, MN: Hazelden.

Hall, P. (2013) *Understanding and Treating Sex Addiction*, Hove: Routledge.

Hazelden Meditations (1989) *Answers in the Heart: Daily Meditations for Men and Women Recovering from Sex Addiction*, Center City, MN: Hazelden.

Milkman, H. and Sunderwirth, S. (2010) *Craving for Ecstasy and Natural Highs*, Los Angeles: Sage.

Penix Sbraga, T. and O'Donohue, W. (2003) *The Sex Addiction Workbook: Proven Strategies to Help You Regain Control of Your Life*, Oakland, CA: New Harbinger.

Zilbergeld, B. (1999) *The New Male Sexuality*, New York: Bantam Books.

The Kick Start Recovery Programme: www.sexaddictionhelp.co.uk.

Online pornography

Carnes, P., Delmonico, D. and Griffin, E. (2008) *In the Shadows of the Net: Breaking Free from Compulsive Online Sexual Behaviour*, Center City, MN: Hazelden.

Maltz, W. and Maltz, L. (2008) *The Porn Trap: The Essential Guide to Overcoming Problems Caused by Pornography*, New York: Harper.

Weiss, R. and Schneider, J. (2006) *Untangling the Web: Sex, Porn and Fantasy Obsession in the Internet Age*, New York: Alyson Books.

Candeo: www.candeobehaviorchange.com.

Your Brain on Porn: www.yourbrainonporn.com.

Paraphilias

Bader, M. (2003) *Arousal: The Secret Logic of Sexual Fantasies*, New York: St Martin's Press.

Baumeister, R. (1989) *Masochism and the Self*, New York: Psychology Press.

Fogel, G. and Myers, W. (eds) (1991) *Perversions and Near-perversions in Clinical Practice: New Psychoanalytic Perspectives*, New Haven, CT: Yale University Press.

Kahr, B. (2007) *Sex and the Psyche*, London: Allen Lane.

Money, J. (1986) *Lovemaps: Clinical Concepts of Sexual/Erotic Health and Pathology, Paraphilia and Gender Transposition in Childhood, Adolescence and Maturity*, New York: Irvington.

Wineberg, T. (1995) *Studies in Dominance and Submission*, Amherst, NY: Prometheus Books.

Women and sex addiction

Carnes, S. (ed.) (2011) *Mending a Shattered Heart: A Guide for Partners of Sex Addicts*, Carefree, AZ: Gentle Path Press.

Collins, G. and Collins, P. (2012) *A Couple's Guide to Sex Addiction*, Avon, MA: Adams.

Davis Kasl, C. (1989) *Women, Sex and Addiction*, New York: Harper and Row.

Mellody, P. (2003) *Facing Codependence*, San Francisco: Harper.

Norwood, R. (2000) *Meditations for Women Who Love Too Much*, London: Arrow Books.

Weiss, D. (2000) *She Has a Secret*, Colorado Springs, CO: Discovery Press.

Love addiction

Mellody, P., Wells Miller, A. and Miller, K. (1992) *Facing Love Addiction: Giving Yourself the Power to Change the Way You Are*, San Francisco: Harper.

Norwood, R. (2008) *Women Who Love Too Much*, London: Arrow Books.

Wilson Schaef, A. (1989) *Escape from Intimacy: The Pseudo-Relationship Addictions*, San Francisco: Harper.

Gay men

Downs, A. (2012) *The Velvet Rage: Overcoming the Pain of Growing up Gay in a Straight Man's World*, Philadelphia, PA: Da Capo Press.

Weiss, R. (2005) *Cruise Control: Understanding Sex Addiction in Gay Men*, New York, Alyson Publications Inc.

Wilson, G. and Rahman, Q. (2005) *Born Gay: The Psychobiology of Sex Orientation*, London: Peter Owen.

Sex addiction and the clergy

Booth, L. (1991) *When God Becomes a Drug*, Los Angeles: Jeremy P. Tarcher, Inc.

Lasser, M. (2004) *Healing the Wounds of Sexual Addiction*, Grand Rapids, MI: Zondervan.

Lockwood. C. (2000) *Falling Forward*, Anaheim, CA: Desert Stream Press.

Shupe, A. (1995) *In the Name of All That Is Holy*, Westport, CT: Praeger.

Thoburn, J. and Baker, R. (eds) (2011) *Clergy Sexual Misconduct: A Systems Approach to Prevention, Intervention and Oversight*, Carefree, AZ: Gentle Path Press.

Resources for partners of sex addicts

Carnes, S. (ed.) (2011) *Mending a Shattered Heart: A Guide for Partners of Sex Addicts*, Carefree, AZ: Gentle Path Press.

Collins, C. and Collins, G. (2012) *A Couple's Guide to Sexual Addiction*, Avon, MA: Adams Media.

Hall, P. (2015) *Sex Addiction: The Partner's Perspective*, London: Routledge.

Steffens, B. and Means, M. (2009) *Your Sexually Addicted Spouse: How Partners Can Cope and Heal*, Far Hills, NJ: New Horizon Press.

Twelve Step programmes

Sex Addicts Anonymous (SAA): www.saa-recovery.org.uk.

Sex and Love Addicts Anonymous (SLAA): www.slaauk.org.

Sexual Compulsives Anonymous (SCA): www.sca-recovery.org.

Sex addiction recovery services

Association for the Treatment of Sexual Addiction and Compulsivity (ATSAC): www.atsac.co.uk.

College of Sexual and Relationship Therapists: www.cosrt.org.uk.

The Hudson Centre: www.thehudsoncentre.co.uk.

International Institute for Trauma and Addiction Professionals (IITAP): www.iitap.com.

The Marylebone Centre for Psychological Therapies: www.marylebonecentre.co.uk and www.sexual-addiction.co.uk.

Paula Hall and Associates: www.paulahall.co.uk.

Relate: www.relate.org.uk.

Bibliography

American Psychiatric Association (APA) (2013) *Diagnostic and Statistical Manual of Mental Disorders*, Fifth Edition, Arlington, VA: American Psychiatric Association.

American Society for Addiction Medicine (ASAM) (no date) 'Definition of addiction'. Online. Available: www.asam.org/for-the-public/definition-of-addiction (accessed 10 November 2013).

Augustine, Saint, Bishop of Hippo (1997, translator Boulding). *The Confessions*, London: Hodder and Stoughton.

Bader, M. (2008) *Arousal: The Secret Logic of Sexual Fantasies*, London: Virgin Books.

Barrett, D. (2010) *Supernormal Stimuli*, New York: W.W. Norton and Company.

Bartholomew, K. and Horowitz, L. (1991) 'Attachment styles among young adults: a test of a four category model', *Journal of Personality and Social Psychology* 61, 2: 226–44.

Baumeister, R. (1991) *Escaping the Self: Alcoholism, Spirituality, Masochism and Other Flights from the Burden of Selfhood*, New York: Basic Books.

Bays, L. and Freeman-Longo, R. (1989) *Why Did I Do it Again: Understanding My Cycle of Problem Behaviors*, Brandon, VT: Safer Society Press.

Beck, J. (1995) *Cognitive Therapy: Basics and Beyond*, New York: Guilford Press.

Bradshaw, J. (2005) *Healing the Shame that Binds You*, Deerfield Beach, FA: Health Communications, Inc.

Byrom, T. (2012) *The Dhammapada: The Sayings of the Buddha*, New York: Vintage Books.

Carnes, P. (1983) *Out of the Shadows*, Minneapolis, MN: CompCare Publishers.

Carnes, P. (1991) *Don't Call It Love*, New York: Bantam Books.

Center on Alcohol, Substance Abuse, and Addictions (CASAA), University of New Mexico (2015) *Personal Values Card*. Online. Available: http://casaa.unm.edu/inst/Personal%20Values%20Card%20Sort.pdf (accessed 8 August 2016).

Ceyhan, A. and Ceyhan, E. (2008) 'Loneliness, depression and computer self-efficacy as predictors of problematic internet use', *CyberPsychology and Behavior: The Impact of the Internet, Multimedia and Virtual Reality on Behaviour and Society* 11, 6: 699–701.

Chaney, M. and Chang, C. (2005) 'A trio of turmoil for internet sexually addicted men who have sex with men: boredom proneness, social connectedness and dissociation', *Sexual Addiction and Compulsivity: The Journal of Treatment and Prevention* 12, 1: 3–18.

Critelli, J. and Bivona, J. (2008) 'Women's erotic rape fantasies: an evaluation of theory and research', *Journal of Sex Research* 45, 1: 57–70.

Fossom, M. and Mason, M. (1986) *Facing Shame: Families in Recovery*, New York: W.W. Norton and Company.

Golding, W. (1980, republished 2013) *Rites of Passage*, London: Faber and Faber.

Goodman, A. (1998) *Sexual Addiction: An Integrated Approach*, Madison, CT: International Universities Press.

Greenberg, D. and Bradford, J. (1997) 'Treatment of the paraphilic disorders: a review of the role of selective serotonin reuptake inhibitors', *Sexual Abuse: A Journal of Research and Treatment* 9, 4: 349–60.

Hall, P. (2013) *Understanding and Treating Sexual Addiction*, London: Routledge.

The Harvard Crimson (2011) '5Qs about pornography with Dr Donald L. Hilton Jr. MD', *The Harvard Crimson*. Online. Available: www.thecrimson.com/2011/4/7/porn-men-addiction-pornography/ (accessed 14 April 2015).

Hilton, D. (2013) 'Pornography addiction – a supranormal stimulus considered in the context of neuroplasticity', *Socioaffective Neuroscience and Psychology* 3, 20767; http://dx.doi.org/10.3402/snp.v3i0.20767 (accessed 12 April 2014).

Hudson-Allez, G. (2009) *Infant Losses, Adult Searches: A Neural and Developmental Perspective on Psychopathology and Sexual Offending*, London: Karnac.

Kafka, M. (1991) 'Successful antidepressant treatment of non-paraphilic sexual addictions and paraphilias in men', *Journal of Clinical Psychiatry* 52, 2: 60–5.

Kafka, M. (1997) 'A monoamine hypothesis for the pathophysiology of paraphilic disorders', *Archives of Sexual Behavior* 26, 4: 343–58.

Kahr, B. (2007) *Sex and the Psyche: The Truth About Our Most Secret Fantasies*, London: Penguin Books.

Katehakis, A. (2016) *Sex Addiction as Affect Dysregulation: A Neurobiologically Informed Holistic Treatment*, New York: W.W. Norton and Company.

Kaufman, G. (1989) *The Psychology of Shame: Theory and Treatment of Shame-Based Syndromes*, New York: Springer Publishing Company.

Kingston, D. and Firestone, P. (2008) 'Problematic hypersexuality: a review of conceptualization and diagnosis', *Sexual Addiction and Compulsivity: The Journal of Prevention and Treatment* 15, 4: 284–310.

Maltz, W. and Maltz, C. (2008) *The Porn Trap: The Essential Guide to Overcoming Problems Caused by Pornography*, New York: Harper Collins.

Milkman, H. and Sunderwirth, S. (2009) *Craving for Ecstasy and Natural Highs: A Positive Approach to Mood Alteration*, Los Angeles: Sage.

Money, J. (1986) *Lovemaps: Clinical Concepts of Sexual/Erotic Health and Pathology, Paraphilia and Gender Transposition in Childhood, Adolescence and Maturity*, Buffalo, NY: Prometheus Books.

Muench, F., Blain, L., Morgenstern, J. and Irwin, T. (2011) 'Self-efficacy and attributions about change in persons attempting to reduce compulsive sexual behavior with medication vs. placebo', *Sexual Addiction and Compulsivity: The Journal of Treatment and Prevention* 18, 4: 232–42.

Nathanson, D. (1992) *Shame and Pride: Affect, Sex and the Birth of the Self*, New York: W.W. Norton and Company.

Padesky, C.A. and Mooney, K.A. (1990) 'Presenting the cognitive model to clients', *International Cognitive Therapy Newsletter* 6: 13–14.

Panksepp, J. (1998) *Affective Neuroscience: The Foundations of Human and Animal Emotions*, Oxford: Oxford University Press.

Pattison, S. (2000) *Shame, Theory, Theology*, Cambridge: Cambridge University Press.

Ray, L. (2012) 'Clinical neuroscience of addiction: applications to psychological science and practice', *Clinical Psychology: Science and Practice* 19, 2: 154–66.

Reynaud, M., Kavila, L., Blecha, L. and Benyamina, A. (2010) 'Is love passion an addictive disorder?' *American Journal of Drug and Alcohol Abuse* 36, 5: 261–7. doi: 10.3109/00952990.2010.495183 (accessed 12 April 2014).

Ryan, F. (2013) *Cognitive Therapy for Addiction: Motivation and Change*, Chichester: Wiley-Blackwell.

Sanders, D. and Wills, F. (2005, reprinted 2006) *Cognitive Therapy: An Introduction*, London: Sage.

Schmitz, J. (2005) 'The interface between impulse-control disorders and addictions: are pleasure pathway responses shared neurobiological substrates?' *Sexual Addiction and Compulsivity: The Journal of Treatment and Prevention* 12: 149–68.

Stephens, E. (2012) *Even Better Than the Real Thing: The Role of Supernormal Stimuli in Unhealthy Behaviours*, PCI College, Dublin. Online. Available: www.pcicollege.ie/even-better-than-the-real-thing (accessed 18 December 2013).

Stoller, R. (1975) *Perversions: The Erotic Form of Hatred*, New York: Pantheon.

Stoller, R. (1987) 'Pornography: daydreams to cure humiliation', in D. Nathanson (ed.) *The Many Faces of Shame*, New York: Guildford Press.

Stop Porn Culture (2014) Online. Available: www.stoppornculture.org (accessed 7 August 2014).

Van Rooij, A., Zinn, M., Schoenmakers, T. and Van de Mheen, D. (2012) 'Treating internet addiction with cognitive behavioural therapy: a thematic analysis of the experience of therapists', *International Journal of Mental Health and Addiction* 10: 69–82.

Veale, D., Ennis, M. and Lambrou, C. (2002) 'Possible association of body dysmorphic disorder with an occupation or education in art and design', *American Journal of Psychiatry* 159, 10: 1788–90.

Verny, T. and Kelly, J. (1981) *The Secret Life of the Unborn Child*, New York: Dell Publishing.

Volkow, N. and Li, T-K. (2005) 'The neuroscience of addiction', *Nature, Neuroscience* 8, 11: 1429–30.

Wainberg, M., Muench, F., Morgenstein, J., Hollander, E., Irwin, T., Parsons, J. *et al.* (2006) 'A double-blind study of Citalopram versus placebo in the treatment of compulsive sexual behaviors in gay and bisexual men', *Journal of Clinical Psychiatry* 67, 12: 1968–73.

Will, D. (1987) 'The sense of shame in psychosis: random comments on shame in the psychotic experience', in D. Nathanson (ed.) *The Many Faces of Shame*, New York: Guildford Press.

Wolf, N. (no date) 'The porn myth', *New York* magazine. Online. Available: http://nymag.com/nymetro/news/trends/n_9437 (accessed 13 April 2014).

Yen, J., Ko, C., Yen, C., Wu, H. and Yang, M. (2007) 'The comorbid psychiatric symptoms of internet addiction: Attention Deficit and Hyperactivity Disorder (ADHD), depression, social phobia and hostility', *Journal of Adolescent Health* 41, 1: 93–8.

Young, K. (2007) 'Cognitive behavior therapy with internet addicts: treatment outcomes and implications', *CyberPsychology and Behavior* 10, 5: 671–9.

Index

Page numbers in **bold** denote figures.

abstinence contract 14
abuse, childhood 30, 46, 84, 86, 90,
  125, 129, 130
accountability partners 9, 165
acting out 6, 98; after-effects 99; build-
  up to 98; point of inevitability 98;
  precursors to 94–6, 105–6; and
  seemingly unimportant decisions
  (SUDs) 97–8, 106; triggers for 97–8,
  106–7
after-effects 99
age 78
alcohol 38, 85, 86, 106, 134, 157
Alcoholics Anonymous 164
alternative activities 136
ambivalence 5–6
American Psychiatric Association
  (APA): *Diagnostic and Statistical
  Manual* 150, 154
American Society of Addictive
  Medicine 41
anger 53
anti-depressant medication 43, 44, 155,
  161
anxiety 53, 94–5, 105, 133–4, 157, 160,
  161
anxious attachment style 46, 47
attachment 46–7, 125
'attack other' mechanism 34
'attack self' mechanism 34
Augustine, Saint 19, 22
auto-asphyxiation 153

automatic thoughts 35, 52, 53, 54
aversion therapy 155
avoidance: as defence against shame 34
avoidant attachment style 46, 47

Barratt, D. 24
Bartholomew, K. 46
Baumeister, R. 21
BDSM practices 153–4
Beck, A. 12
bedwetting 125
behaviours 53; and values 62
Ben case example: cycle of addiction
  99–101; precursors to acting out 94–5
biological drive 38–41
birth stories 87–8, 124–5
black and white thinking 116
blaming others 33, 114, 115
blaming self 115, 119
body dysmorphic disorder 34
boredom 18, 39, 94, 95, 105, 108–9,
  151, 160, 162
Bradshaw, J. 28
brain: executive function 39; plasticity
  44–5; and repetitious learning 40,
  44–5; reward system 40–1
brain chemistry 37, 41–4, 80, 168
breath play 153
build-up phase 98
bullying 125

career consequences 69

rationalisation 113–14
reconstitution phase 99
reflective self 6, **7**
relapse prevention 133–45; worksheet
    139–43
relationship therapy 138
relationships: consequences for 71,
    151–2; improving quality of 137–8;
    over-controlling partners in 97–8
religion 38, 86, 159
religious leaders: as sources of help 9
residential treatment 166
reward 95
Robert case example, values
    clarification 63
Robin case example, family of origin
    86–7
Roderick case example: precursors to
    acting out 95
Roger case example: provisional sex
    plan 81
'romance addiction' 158
romantic attraction 38–9, 168
Rupert case example: exiting the cycle
    of addiction 107–8

sado-masochism 153–4
Sanders, D. 116
school experiences 125
secure attachment style 46
seemingly unimportant decisions
    (SUDs) 96–7, 106
selective serotonin reuptake inhibitors
    (SSRIs) 43, 44, 155
self-blame 115, 119, 120
self-care 21–2
self-esteem 21, 166
self-image, impact on 71
self-soothing 40, 44, 45, 47, 51
self-worth 21
serotonin 37, 41, 43, 44
serving others 138
Sex Addicts Anonymous (SAA) 8–9,
    131, 136, 137, 164, 165
Sex and Love Addicts Anonymous
    (SLAA) 8–9, 136, 164, 165
sex workers 25, 78
Sexaholics Anonymous (SA) 164–5

sexual addiction 13, 19–22; ten signs of
    20
sexual templates 79, 80, 125, 169
sexualised family environments 86–7,
    89
sexually transmitted infections (STIs)
    68–9
shame 27–36, 53, 55, 69–70, 134, 152,
    157, 160, 161; defences against
    33–4, 113–15; defining 27–9; healing
    of 34–6; as precursor to acting out
    94, 95; and sexual addiction 29–33
Shame (film) 36, 70
shame compass 115
shame museum exercise 90–1
shame spiral 33
social consequences 68, 71–2
sponsors 9, 165
Stephens, E. 24
stigmatisation 169
Stoller, R. 29
'Stop It Now' helpline 153
Strauss-Kahn, D. 39
stress 42, 132, 136, 161
substance use 40, 157–8; *see also*
    alcohol
supernormal stimuli 23–6, 78, 150–1

therapy: individual 9–10, 137, 163–4;
    see also cognitive behavioural
    therapy
thinking errors *see* cognitive distortions
Thomas case example, family of origin
    87
time wasted 69, 70
Tinbergen, N. 23–4, 26
trauma egg exercise 89–90, **91**
triggers 97–8, 106–7
Twelve Step programmes 8–9, 136–7,
    164–5, 166

underage people, sexual attraction to 80
unrealistic expectations 118
urge diary 16–18

values clarification 61–6; exercise 63–5
vasopressin 37, 41, 42
Verny, T. 88
Volkow, N. 38

T - #0065 - 301020 - C0 - 216/138/10 - PB - 9781138925342 - Matt Lamination